AF352603

A Longhouse Fragmented

A Longhouse Fragmented

Ohio Iroquois Autonomy in the Nineteenth Century

Brian Joseph Gilley

State University of New York Press

Published by
STATE UNIVERSITY OF NEW YORK PRESS, ALBANY

For information, contact
State University of New York Press, Albany, NY
www.sunypress.edu

Production, Laurie Searl
Marketing, Anne M. Valentine

Library of Congress Cataloging-in-Publication Data

Gilley, Brian Joseph, 1972–
    A longhouse fragmented : Ohio Iroquois autonomy in the nineteenth century /
Brian Joseph Gilley.
        pages cm.
    Includes bibliographical references and index.
    ISBN 978-1-4384-4939-5 (hardcover : alk. paper)
    1. Iroquois Indians—Ohio—History—19th century. 2. Iroquois Indians—Ohio—Politics and government. 3. Iroquois Indians—Ohio—Social life and customs. I. Title.

E99.I7G52 2014
977.1004'9755—dc23   2013003398

10 9 8 7 6 5 4 3 2 1

CONTENTS

Illustrations

Preface

At the Fiftieth Annual Conference on Iroquois Research in 1995, I found myself among some of the most important people in Native North American anthropology, archaeology, and history. Students with direct intellectual lineages to Franz Boas mingled with fledgling scholars and graduate students such as me. Fortunately, Laurence Hauptman had taken me under his wing, and he ushered me to meet various Iroquois scholars. Unlike the other graduate students, I was encouraged to sit at the dinner table with William Fenton, Floyd Lounsbury, Elisabeth Tooker, and William Sturtevant as well as the equally well-known generation of Iroquois scholars after them. I got to share a six-pack with Dean Snow and Bill Sturtevant in the dormitory of the Rennselaerville Institute, where the conference was held. Only now do I realize how fortunate I was to have access to such outstanding scholars for an entire weekend and how frequently I embarrassed myself with my naiveté and overconfidence in the importance of my own research. I presented a paper on the Seneca-Cayuga of Oklahoma and sought the consultation of Drs. Sturtevant and Tooker, who were among the few living scholars to have conducted ethnohistorical and ethnographic research with the Seneca-Cayuga. During my audience with Sturtevant and Tooker, they summarized what they had written about the community and gave me advice on where to look for documents. However, the spark for my research project came in the last few minutes of our conversation when Sturtevant said, to my best recollection, "Those Western people are not Iroquois as we think of the Six Nations. They have kinship, a longhouse, but they're not actually Iroquois." Throughout the weekend of papers and celebrations in honor of the fiftieth conference, a particular idea about what is Iroquois and what qualifies as legitimate Iroquois research began to emerge.

Over the years I visited Sturtevant at the Smithsonian a few times and talked about the Seneca-Cayuga and other displaced Iroquois. I had the chance to talk with Fenton and Tooker about the project a few years after the conference as well. In all instances, the scholars I encountered wanted to understand more about the peoples to the west who count their cultural and historical origins among the Six Nations, but they were unwilling to put them socially, culturally, or politically on equal footing. In the course of the research leading to the publication of this book, I have become acutely aware of the ways in which Iroquois studies has invested in a kind of hegemonic control of "Iroquois," "Six Nations," and the content of those cultures. I am not implying a grand academic conspiracy meant to prevent new scholarship or the development of the field. Rather, I only experienced encouragement from these founding scholars. At the same time, after I completed the research on the Seneca of Sandusky, of whom the Oklahoma Seneca-Cayuga are descendent, I encountered numerous obstacles to publishing the work. Certainly my initial critiques of Iroquois studies reflected the immaturity of my scholarship, but the ethnohistorical evidence supported the probability of Iroquois studies' unfortunate dismissal of the Western peoples. Reviewer critiques of my submissions to journals outright dismissed the possibility of an "authentic" Iroquois society in the Ohio Valley in the nineteenth century. Their argument against my interpretation was two-fold: first, the Ohio Territory peoples were not engaged with the settler state as a nation or a "league"; and second, their movement west in the eighteenth century displaced them from the metaphorical longhouse that extended across New York. There was a clear interest in solidifying what could be called Iroquois despite the influence of exceptional scholarly works such as Richard White's *The Middle Ground* and Michael McConnell's *A Country Between*, which provide an alternative interpretation for the sociopolitical relevance of the Western Iroquois and Algonquian peoples. Discouraged by the reception of my ethnohistorical work, I abandoned the Seneca of Sandusky project for over a decade until reading the introduction to Jon Parmenter's *The Edge of the Woods*, which was ironically the subtitle for the fiftieth anniversary Iroquois conference I first attended.[1]

Parmenter eloquently and meticulously presents many of the issues that have long bothered scholars of Native America about Iroquois studies, such as its provincialism and unwillingness to incorporate itself into broader conceptualizations of native studies. The arguments in *The Edge of the Woods* center on the Iroquois sociopolitical tendency to use transitional spaces as socially restorative and as catalysts for cultural change while emphasizing continuity with the basic values of the Longhouse. Parmenter does something no other scholar has done—he links the fundamental values of the Deganawidah Epic, which is the conceptual foundation for the League, to actual everyday ways of being Iroquois. Additionally, he uses the Deganawidah Epic as a critique of an academically produced, geographically sedentary Iroquois and the ways academics place spatial boundaries on the sociopolitical history of the Six Nations. Some of my critiques of Iroquois studies mirror those of Parmenter; at the same time, I seek to make an argument explicitly linking a temporal and geographic Iroquois exceptionalism. In doing so, I hope to disentangle the analytical usefulness of our most fundamental knowledge about the Iroquois from the inherent limitations of Iroquois particularism. I use the history of the Ohio Iroquois, specifically the people known as the Sandusky Seneca, to understand how cultural logics are spatially mobile and temporally durable. Thus the arguments and evidence presented here will seek to show how a small group of Iroquois, the people known as the Sandusky Seneca, continued to make use of the fundamental logics of the Longhouse despite occupying a different geographic space than their Six Nations relatives.

Examining this problem requires illustrating both the logic of the Longhouse and that of Iroquois studies. Both converge at various moments in the actual history of Iroquois peoples and at crucial moments in academic knowledge production. As scholars can draw a line of continuity from precontact proto-Iroquois societies to the present community practices of twenty-first-century Iroquois, we can also map a continuity of settler logics from protoethnographic colonial accounts to Lewis Henry Morgan and well into the theoretically sophisticated works published today. Likewise we can draw a line of continuity between the sociopolitical foundations of Iroquois culture to the people who would come to be known as the Seneca of Sandusky and later the Seneca-Cayuga of Oklahoma.

Revisiting this topic is also motivated by a Seneca-Cayuga woman I met through my ethnographic research on Two-Spirit people. When I met Jennifer (a pseudonym) about ten years ago, she was in her early twenties and had recently taken one of my Cherokee friends and ethnographic consultants as a brother through adoption. During my time of seeing her on a regular basis, she spoke about the ceremonies at Turkey Ford, the ceremonial grounds established by the Seneca of Sandusky after removal to the Cowskin River on the Neosho Reservation, Indian Territory. She always represented "proof" of my argument for cultural continuity. In late 2008 I saw her again; this time she had a tattoo of the Haudenosaunee flag, which graphically represents the original Five Nations using squares and an Eastern white pine connected by a single line. I asked her about the tattoo, and she replied that she was showing her "Haudenosaunee pride." In an ethnographic moment, I asked her about the feelings she had about the Six Nations. She replied that "we are all part of a single longhouse extending across Turtle Island." Her response was a little too canned and "Indian pride" for me, so I probed some more. She told me about her and her family's reconnection with Seneca relatives in New York. Her family had started traveling to New York when they could for family reunions and large annual ceremonies. She was being inducted into a ceremonial community at Cattaraugus and was keeping up with family and friends she made there through Facebook. When I implied that this was an attempt at some kind of "return," she expressed an annoyance at the notion of the Six Nations somehow validating her sense of Haudenosaunee-ness. For her, the Seneca-Cayuga community was simply an extension of a larger Haudenosaunee community spread throughout the United States, in which she also included urban Mohawks in New York City and Canadian Iroquois.

After I returned from my trip to Oklahoma and my conversation with Jennifer, I dug out the accordion files containing my research on the Seneca of Sandusky. Near the top of the pile were the notes I had taken during an interview with a Seneca-Cayuga elder in the mid-1990s. Prompted by William Sturtevant's claim to me that the Seneca and Cayuga of the Seneca-Cayuga thought of themselves as different people, I asked that elder, Ellen (a pseudonym), more than a decade ago, about any distinction between the two affiliations among her community. She replied that people thought of themselves and spoke of themselves as Seneca-Cayuga, not Seneca or Cayuga. People had intermarried, particularly with the Cherokee, but continued to refer to themselves as mixed "Seneca-Cayuga" and "Cherokee." Ellen told me the story of removal (told in chapters two and three in this book) and of the contentious times during the mid-1950s termination debate, which produced an intense factionalism among the Seneca-Cayuga. The crisis of the 1950s saw a group of Seneca-Cayuga calling themselves the Western Cayuga. This group was backed by the descendants of Sandusky Seneca headman Splitlog.[2] Even during this difficult time, Ellen was adamant about the community dealing with its issues through a commitment to its values. She did not use the term *Great Law of Peace* or any other ethnohistorical or ethnographic terms. But in my notes about our conversation these principles show through in her explanation of how the community held councils on difficult topics and continued to hold ceremony and function as a society. She rejected the idea of factionalism and instead used the idea of intrafamily conflict to illustrate the ways the Seneca-Cayuga community dealt with the difficulties of being colonized peoples.

If I was to seek a postcolonial-oriented argument based on continuity and have it be legitimate in the eyes of scholars, I realized I needed to seek out the origins of cultural persistence and deliberate change. Therefore, the argument about continuity, change, and persistence in this book focuses on the need to revise how we come to understand native communities as topics of inquiry and people about whom we produce knowledge. In my mind, the argument for recognizing change and continuity is both an act of refusing perspectives fragmenting native history from contemporary societies and a form of recognition of the sociopolitical power of native self-directed thought and action. Revisiting the Seneca of Sandusky project seemed the perfect way to begin a methodological conversation and recognize the potential in a geographic and cultural space of inquiry seemingly forgotten by academics. Because this book is intended to begin a conversation, it is short on purpose and will hopefully illustrate the potential for research using more recent and emergent approaches. In finally getting this project into a cohesive set of ideas and documentation, I owe thanks to a few key people who helped influence the end product. I am grateful to Laurence Hauptman for introducing me to the project over a decade ago. I am also grateful to Morris Foster for teaching me an alternative way of reading documents and understanding social organization among American Indians. I am grateful to the founders of Iroquois studies who gave me their time, especially William Sturtevant, Elizabeth Tooker, and William Fenton, may they rest in peace. A few colleagues have also greatly influenced this project. Benjamin Eastman sat through numerous discussions of postcolonial theory and helped guide my application of its key concepts to the Sandusky data. Cameron Wesson provided insights on the colonial encounter in the Americas as well as encouragement for the methodological challenges of writing this book. My esteemed colleagues Christina Snyder, Matt Guterl, Eduardo Brondizio, Ray DeMallie, and Jacob Lee all provided encouragement at moments when I needed to discuss ideas and challenges. I am thankful to the staff at the Glenn Black Lab at Indiana University Bloomington (IUB) for their help with resources.

Personal thanks go to Mary Connors, my assistant at the First Nations Center at IUB, for taking up the slack when I needed her. My wife, Caroline, was always willing to listen to my verbose meanderings on the project and correct my grammar. My children—Aurianna, Parker, and Joseph—are supportive in ways they do not even know. No amount of thanks will express my gratitude to my family.

INTRODUCTION

Francis Jennings refers to the "imaginary" Iroquois as the product of two moments in North American colonial and US history. The first came as the result of British attempts to bring Iroquoian peoples and their territories under the empire's sphere of influence in the seventeenth and eighteenth centuries. Through historiographies by British colonial intellectuals, this project produced the idea of a supreme and powerful Iroquois empire that controlled land and people from Canada to the Deep South and as far West as Illinois.[1] Providing the politically advantageous link between the British Empire and the empire of the Iroquois, this publicity campaign was designed to inform colonial competitors, specifically the French, that anywhere the Six Nations extended their influence was actually under British imperial control by proxy. As British control over the Northeast began to wane in the mid-1700s and with Britain's defeat in the American Revolutionary War, the myth of Six Nations supremacy and its purpose began to fall apart. However, the mystique of the great Iroquois Nation remained a crucial aspect of American history through the twentieth century. The political history of the Iroquois was so integrally linked to the birth of the United States that they are credited with providing the model for the American state.[2] Intellectual appreciation for the Iroquois as a well-organized nation with a clear statelike purpose, as well as national-level practices and cultural patterns, also continues to perpetuate their mythic status by distinguishing the historic Six Nations from any other American Indian society. According to Jennings, Iroquois tradition and the birth of American anthropology converged in the work of Northeast intellectuals in the nineteenth century to create the second moment, where "The double movement from a single source is hidden behind the reemergence of the Iroquois tradition as fact determined by the fledgling science of anthropology."[3] With two different methodologies and a shared social agenda, Lewis Henry Morgan produced ethnographic modules and Francis Parkman crafted idealized portraits of the Iroquois people, their culture and social practices. Using social evolution, both men were engaged in an ongoing intellectual battle to define what the Iroquois, and natives in general, meant in American social history, science, and public policy. In the work of Parkman and Morgan we find the roots of the second moment, the 'empirical' Iroquois—an idea divorced from the lived moments of people; a people whose academic history, and to an extent their community history, was settled by the knowledge that has been and continues to be produced about them.

In the preface to *League of the Ho-de'-no-sau-nee*, Lewis Henry Morgan asked, "Can the residue of the Iroquois be reclaimed, and finally be raised to the position of citizens of the State?" For Morgan the citizenship to which he was referring is the legal classification of a person with rights and responsibilities under the state while at the same time, and of greater concern, was the state as a set of national characteristics associated with the United States of America. For Morgan the most important question was, to what extent could the Iroquois and other Indians be considered partners in the nation and in the civil society American nationalism purported to support? In answering this question, according to Daniel Moses, Morgan "converted nostalgia into an undercover radicalism based on the assumption at the foundation of his work: because what was, is no longer, what is cannot remain the same . . . he predicted a revival, in a new form, of the 'liberty, equality, and fraternity' which he believed existed among primitive peoples."[4] Unlike his politically progressive social compatriots, many of whom were engaged in continual hand wringing over what to do with the country's Others, Morgan sought to discover the ways in which American Indians, specifically the Iroquois, could contribute and already had contributed to the pluralistic nation. For some Americans, the Indian was an impediment to the realization of Manifest Destiny; to the more conservative settler classes of the South and Mid-Atlantic regions, he was inherently inferior. However, Morgan subscribed to a belief both nationalist and naturalistic, scientific but fully caught up in American romanticism. Paul van der Grijp sees Morgan's "untaught anthropology" as the "inseparable triplet" of science, commerce, and democracy, according to which Indian policy had to provide for the Indian "to be incorporated into the great brotherhood of American nations as equal citizens; perhaps even be engrafted to our race."[5] The first step in addressing the schism between America's primitives and its progress was placing the Iroquois in the middle of his

Social Darwinist scheme of development—just above the bottom so as to not be irredeemable but not so near the top as to be competitive with whites. The second step was the accumulation of ethnographic data detailing the complexity of premodern and contemporary Iroquois society as a way to justify the Iroquois' relatively high ranking. Through this ethnographic work Morgan was able to illustrate the various ways in which the Iroquois were made of fine human stock with the potential for civilization and thus ready-made for the absorption of American nationalism. At the same time, the Indian could not overcome his own historiography, his pigment, and his features in a phenotypically obsessed sociopolitical world. Therefore, Morgan's ethnographies also served to classify natives and ready the American citizenry for the integration of geographically near native Others into civil society through what Robert Wiebe refers to as the "search for order" in the foundations of the Progressive Era.[6] Morgan's search for order helped bring the geographically near Native into the Nation through description, catalog and epistemological construction. The "ordering" of observational data about the Iroquois would have significant ramifications for the ways in which all succeeding generations of scholars framed research questions, native community engagement, and the degree to which new ideas are allowed into the field.

Knowledge about the Iroquois, as the founders of democracy and the first subject of anthropology, has almost exclusively come from what Partha Chatterjee characterizes as the domain of the "outside," which is "of the economy and of state-craft, of science and technology," the domain where the imperialist has to continually prove its superiority to the colonized. The outside is distinct from the domain of the "inner" or "spiritual," which "bears the essential marks of cultural identity" embodied in cultural institutions such as religion, kinship, and gender relations. The "inside," which exists in the locally guarded and daily used social elements and cultural logics, becomes fragmented from the nation through interactions with the settler state. Practices as well as the people engaging in the practices become fragmented away from the "outside" because their cultural conservatism is of little use to colonial and settler administrators. The "outside" in the form of colonial relations between the Iroquois and the conglomeration of European powers in the Northeast New World—Dutch, French, British—overpowers understanding of the ways in which the institutions of the "inside" remain the most resistant to change and are preserved by their limited use for colonial administrative logic. Thus, to be incorporated into the nationalist state, the "original" peoples who came with the land must socially, politically, and, as I argue, epistemologically fit into the nation.[7] The intellectual roots of Iroquois studies co-opted the "inner" of Iroquois to support the documentation of the Six Nations—not as a group of living people but as an emblem of a specific way of producing knowledge about American Indian culture history and the American nation. Imagining Indians through play, policy, and ethnographic writing, as Deloria points out, was "a way of imagining new American identities, meaningful in relation to the successful Revolution, the emerging market economy, and the new governments and political parties busy consolidating and distributing power across the landscape."[8] Academic knowledge produced by anthropology and history about the Iroquois supported an epistemological way of imagining social relations that prioritized "democratic" values in keeping with the tendency to rank societies, races, and ethnicities according to their degree of civilization. The Iroquois Nation as an entity evolved out of "successive social necessities developing out of contradictions in prior stages or eras" explicitly articulated with U.S. political and social understanding.[9]

As Audra Simpson points out, the accounts of culture allow Empire to document "a difference that had been contained into neat, ethnically-defined territorial spaces that now needed to be made sense of, to be ordered, ranked, to be governed, to be possessed."[10] The study of the outside Iroquois—of a temporally and spatially constructed contact era and early colonial Six Nations democratic polity—has the effect of undermining the history of the ways in which fundamental cultural logics embedded in undifferentiated social elements are maintained and reproduced across temporal and spatial boundaries.[11] It undermines the durability of cultural institutions and practices for any other sake than nationhood and colonial patrimony. The narrative of the epistemological Iroquois locates social continuity in sustained and continual knowledge produced within the American Indian episteme, where the maintenance of cultural forms is explained through a universalized historiography but simultaneously bounded within a social history independent of the self-directed cultural changes experienced by the living Iroquois peoples. The boundaries of Iroquois nation and place are reproduced in the textual understanding of their social organization and their importance as the "first object" of American anthropology.[12]

In practical terms for documenting and learning from social history, the epistemological Iroquois diverts our attention from the possibilities of "other" forms of Iroquoisness; from the possibility that individuals who locate their personal and social history among the colonial-era Iroquois but have ceased to occupy that physical and cultural space maintain a legitimate connection to that past. Eventually the stories of the fragments—cultural conservatives who are spatially mobile—"recede from the official narrative . . . and are consigned to being no more than the irrational cultural substrate of the rationalizing modern state."[13] The construction of the modern indigenous state produces as an effect a set of fragments, of outliers to which little attention is paid until the shoring up of colonial difference (the difference between the indigenous nation and the colonizer) is required. "Iroquois" exists in two manifestations, the actual sovereign people who occupy social, cultural, and political space and the Iroquois of the epistemological imagination. While these two converge at various moments in history and play off one another in contemporary identity politics, I am concerned with the construction of the epistemological Iroquois from fragments (various local practices normalized by ethnoscience) and the human fragments created by the settler-directed construction of the native as it was needed to historically ground American colonialism.

There are two methodological effects of the institution of the epistemological Iroquois. First there is the conflation of Iroquois into "settlement" epistemologies by unifying community with the nation. Chatterjee tells us: "But community is not easily appropriated within the narrative of [the colonizer]. Community, from the latter's standpoint, belongs to the domain of the natural, the primordial. Only in its sanitized, domesticated form can it become a shared subjective feeling that protects and nurtures. But it always carries with it the threatening possibility of becoming violent, divisive, fearsome, irrational."[14] Thus the communities who translocated to the western frontier (Ohio Territory) in the late eighteenth century away from the Iroquois proper represent the primordial, nonnationalized and thus illegitimate embodiment of Iroquois culture. These translocated people are more difficult to "order" within epistemological particularities and thus occupy a secondary historical and intellectual space. The second effect is an intellectual institutional disguise for the ways in which community potentially challenges settlement on its own terms; the ways in which non-Western cultural logics cut and dodge the rigors of colonialism and how native practice is mobile through the durable cultural thoughts and practices of indigenous peoples.

LOCALS, NATIONS, NATIVES

During the early part of the twentieth century there was a great debate over the exact origins of the Iroquois. H. M. Lloyd along with Lewis Henry Morgan had postulated a Western origin for the Iroquois. These early antiquarian enthusiasts found it difficult to believe that the Iroquois had developed their skill for agriculture and complex ceremonial and kinship structure while they were in the Northeast. Arthur C. Parker and others speculated that the Iroquois had originated in the Mississippi Valley, where they learned about agriculture from chiefdom societies. Iroquois groups were thought to have migrated to New York State and pushed out the Algonquian in the 1500s, shortly before contact with Europeans. For their settlement tendencies and complexity of social institutions, Morgan had placed the Iroquois Confederacy at the highest possible location for "inferior races" in his evolutionary ladder. For Morgan, however, the elevated position of the Iroquois required a socio-cultural and more importantly a biological origin outside the Northeast. Physical and social migration from more sophisticated origins fit nicely into the overall Social Darwinist attitudes of the time and provided an ideal counterpoint for scholars concerned with overturning legacies of ethnocentricism in science and history.[15]

Nearly a century after Morgan, William Fenton's (1940) article "Problems Arising from the Historic North-Eastern Position of the Iroquois" continued to grapple with the mysteries of Northeast native society: "a major problem of Iroquois research shall be to explain their intrusive linguistic and cultural position in the northeast."[16] A Boasian by training, Fenton did not subscribe to Morgan's Social Darwinist ideas, but rather employed a diffusionist approach to speculate a Southeastern geographic and cultural origin for the Iroquois. Diffusionist perspectives would stand until Richard MacNeish's 1952 monograph *Iroquois Pottery Types* challenged prominent migration theories to argue that the Iroquois had evolved from prehistoric occupations of New York and Ohio. What has come to be known as the "in situ theory" proposes an Iroquois culture with roots in Hopewellian traditions and Pre-Columbian origins in the Northeast. More important about MacNeish's in situ hypothesis was his challenge to the Social Darwinist legacy in Iroquois archaeology, which essentially ended the search for Iroquois "origins." His first accomplishment was to show continuity from pre-historic Northeastern cultures to the historic Iroquois based on the same pottery attributes used to promote migration theories. Second, and more importantly, by successfully challenging social evolutionary models, MacNeish transformed the ways that academic archaeologists thought about the "local" in the Northeast.[17] Fenton's migration theory did not hold up under MacNeish's in situ. Instead, Fenton's notion of "localism" foreshadowed MacNeish's proposition and continues as a foundational part of our cultural-historical understanding of Iroquois social organization. Fenton had a "growing conviction that the Iroquois town or settlement, in fact the local group, bears all the seeds out of which more elaborate tribal and intertribal institutions have grown. If the town and the band are synonymous, if the local group is the unit of Iroquois culture, it is important to know how many there were and where they were situated during different periods." Localism was, for Fenton, the fundamental social basis upon which the League was founded. The local was where the maintenance work of ceremony, kinship, language, and politics for Iroquois society occurred. Metaphorically, "they [the Iroquois] referred to the confederacy as if they had erected a longhouse together" . . . the greater part of their domain was devoid of habitation, for their towns, situated on hills away from streams, were strung along an east-west trail which was the hallway through the longhouse. . . . It was this league of ragged villages."[18] The local was and continues to be important to the Iroquois and all social, political, and economic relations emanating from lineage, clan, and community. I am not questioning Fenton's accurate representation of the importance placed on the local by Iroquois peoples, which is a phenomenon found throughout Native America. The problem is how localism, when married to in situ, acted as epistemological grounding for seeing continuity in the New York Iroquois and discontinuity elsewhere. Epistemologies act as signposts for determining who and where "counts" as Iroquois. I am asking, how have these ideas produced customary epistemological practices through the conflation of place of residence, racial and ethnic identity, and tribal affiliation?

As two of the most influential ideas in Northeast native studies, Fenton's localism and MacNeish's in situ left untouched the late-liberal-humanist political agenda of Morgan and foreshadowed its reproduction throughout twentieth-century Iroquois scholarship. At the heart of localism's and in situ's unchallenged nationalism is the "naturalization" of natives into the settler citizens' nativeness, that is of native-born Americans of European ancestry.[19] Prizing the local as geographically stable, rather than the portable social institutions of native peoples, also suggests "that the romance of spatial confinement was that it contrasted 'the native's' supposed enchantment, tradition, culture and simplicity with the ethnographer's spatial mobility, which stood for enlightenment, modernity, science and development."[20] The in situ and "localized" Iroquois could maintain a premodern but fully nationalist existence through the documentation of Iroquois studies. For the nineteenth-century "emigrant" Iroquois, who for scholars look far too much like settlers in their movements into the Ohio and Indian Territories and dislocalized in their spatial mobility, an exclusion from the processes of documentation in the twentieth century was inevitable. The intellectual foundations and continuing twentieth-century products of Iroquois studies "stressed one possible outcome of culture contact for the future" of the displaced Iroquois peoples, which "was to be a time when Indians—politically, linguistically and culturally—would become indistinguishable from other Americans" on the frontier.[21] Even with the twentieth-century intellectual transition from stressing cultural loss to analysis that emphasized oppression, colonialism, sovereignty, resistance, and the like, academics remain largely uninterested in these groups of natives who had already somewhat "disappeared" from the landscape of inquiry. In the nineteenth century, as the epistemological Iroquois became increasingly the products of settler intellectualism, the people who "lived Iroquois" every day away from the Iroquois "proper" increasingly became the subjects of state apparatus designed for dealing with the "Indian problem." By Fenton and MacNeish's time, the Ohio Territory was the state of Ohio and the native people who had occupied that landscape had been moved westward into Indian Territory.

SOCIAL UNITS, ANALYSIS, AND METHOD

The story of the Ohio Iroquois is made difficult by the inconsistency of documents for certain periods, the general way in which Ohio Indians were referred to as "Mingo," "Savage," or "Indians," and the frequent movement of people in and out of the Ohio Valley. Decades of Ohio Iroquois activities are missing from the historic record, and when they do appear in any significant way it is often as the result of attempted treaty negations, land cessions, or surrounding acts of colonial aggression. Not until the late eighteenth and early nineteenth centuries do we begin to see the rich, but biased, settler accounts of Ohio Iroquois culture, political structure, and lifeways. Thus any study of the Ohio Iroquois will have informational gaps in the history of communities and the lives of major sociopolitical figures.

As one can imagine, the sparseness of documents for certain periods has yet to inspire a significant academic interest in the Ohio peoples other than the Ottawa, Wyandotte, and Shawnee, whose military and political exploits generated a significant amount of documentation. Furthermore, during the early to mid-nineteenth century, the Southeastern peoples, such as the Cherokee, were absorbing the majority of national interest and political attention in critical periods for people in the Ohio Valley, who were dealing with the effects of Manifest Destiny as well. The attention toward the Southeast and the political engagement by larger, more aggressive communities in Ohio led to underdocumentation for the Ohio Iroquois. Until the treaties of the early nineteenth century, information on the Ohio Iroquois must be mined out of correspondence, diary entries, treaty negotiations, traveler accounts, and the records of trading posts. Some accounts do not name Iroquois groups explicitly, and the social identity of a community, town, or settlement must be cross-validated with other documents.

It is not until the documents around the time of the Battle of Fallen Timbers in 1794 that a distinct Ohio Iroquois community comes into focus. In the beginning of the nineteenth century, however, the documentation begins to distinguish Ohio communities both geographically and culturally from one another. Indian agent letters, missionary reports, and settler diaries replace more general terms about Ohio Indians, Ohio Iroquois, or "Mingo" with more specific terms such as Seneca of Sandusky or Mixed Shawnee-Seneca. Such designations, while not always tribal, provided settlers of the area and government officials with designations representing a variety of community characteristics such as geographic location, leadership, and culture. For example, letters discussing the Seneca Mixed Band referred to the Seneca and Shawnee community near Lewistown, Ohio. Distinguishing between communities was no doubt a reflection of the US government's interest in obtaining Ohio Indian lands, an administrative need to change types of interactions with communities, and the political need to identify individuals with whom to negotiate cessions. The need to distinguish communities, however, provides better documentation for individual villages, leaders, and sociopolitical happenings. By the War of 1812 and the treaty negotiations following it, two distinct "Seneca" communities are recognized in the documents, one on the Upper Sandusky and another in Lewistown. The Sandusky community is the better documented and lends itself to a community-based approach to social history.

Two issues of methodology both emerge and are resolved by the historic documentation of the Ohio Iroquois. First, the inconsistency of 'evidence' prevents us from reconstructing a detailed accounting of Iroquois 'tribal' identities in Ohio, and as such a traditional historical analysis of community identity is difficult. It is also difficult to account for Ohio Iroquois individuals, lineages, and micro-level activities during certain periods, specifically in the pre-1817 period, prior to the reservation. Additionally, the historian of the Iroquois, and of Native America in general, will be quite uncomfortable with the inconsistencies in the documents, such as the nebulousness created by settler and agent use of "Seneca," "Iroquois," and "Indians" interchangeably to refer to the peoples occupying the Upper Sandusky region as well as the tendency to use the term "Six Nations" to refer to the Iroquois living in Ohio, not the New York Iroquois.

In the absence of consistency in the documents, and of the individuals who generated them, inference is required, which inches ever closer to the fringes of historical methodology. The documentation on the Ohio Iroquois, however, requires the researcher to use provenance and other details to connect sources back to the community in discussion. Changing the units of analysis from "identity" to "community" also allows us to expand our understanding of Iroquois social organization beyond the "tribe" or nation and challenges us to recognize the other potentially important ways natives were organizing sociopolitically. My approach is to prioritize the well documented social units, which happen to be the social units we see the Sandusky people using, such as the community longhouse. This shift not only allows an analysis prevented by the most conservative forms of Iroquois studies, it is also in keeping with my argument that identities such as Seneca and Mohawk and their geographic placement may not be the most important to the actual people or the most important to my particular analysis.

The second problem is one of 'authenticity' for the Ohio Iroquois, which arises from the issues described above but also as an effect of a methodological controversy over upstreaming. William Fenton, the originator of upstreaming, used it as an ethnohistorical tool to fill in gaps left by poor historic documentation. Fenton's "historical upstreaming" was founded on the premise that "major patterns of culture remain stable over long periods of time, producing repeated uniformities" and "these patterns can best be seen by proceeding from the known ethnological present to the unknown past."[22] Upstreaming in its initial form helped to reorient the role of history and historical documentation in anthropology as well as helping to challenge various ethnocentric tenets within American Indian studies. Fenton and others were able to illustrate a level of sociocultural continuity between the communities of the mid-twentieth century and those of the early republic all the way to precontact. By the late 1950s upstreaming had become a critical research tool in historical anthropology, ethnohistory, and archaeology. Upstreaming also provided the evidence needed to bolster land claims and enforce treaty negotiations in the termination era and later in tribal recognition cases of the mid- and late twentieth century. The unfortunate byproduct of upstreaming, according to Kurt Jordan, was a kind of "melancholic" search for authenticity and inauthenticity; that is, Fenton's original methodology was attempting to discern the more "authentic traditional" from the "degenerate modern" by seeking similarities between the ethnographic present and the documented past "focusing only on traditions that remained consistent for decades or even centuries, in the process excluding large swaths of Iroquois experience from scholarly research."[23] The evidence of continuous traditions was then used to create histories which, according to Richard White in *The Middle Ground*, were biased toward continuity. The effect of this bias is the orientation of sociopolitical arrangements according to broadly conceived notions of tribe or nation, which White challenges in his work by showing the ways communities in the Ohio Valley were formed and dissolved through complex cultural apparatuses, such as kinship.[24] At issue for scholars such as White and Jordan are the ways a "constricted definition of authenticity limits 'the Iroquois cultural heritage' to those aspects of Iroquois life amenable to upstreaming, in the process excluding all cultural practices . . . that contained "demonstrable" European influence, regardless of the degree to which they manifested indigenous roots or operated within contexts controlled by Native logics."[25]

In an alternative to upstreaming and the search for an authentic version of Eastern Indians in Ohio, White argues for a space of "accommodation" between different actors—between colonized and colonizer as well as the mutually colonized—where new meanings and practices are produced. These accommodations are the result of desires, misunderstandings, and to some degree the consequences of mutual fault. In the twentieth-anniversary edition of *The Middle Ground*, White further argues: "A middle ground is the creation, in part through creative misunderstanding, of a set of practices, rituals, offices and beliefs that although comprised of elements of the group in contact is as a whole separate from the practices and beliefs of all of those groups." Accordingly in White's logic, the Ohio Territory lacked a coherent social organization, because it lacked infrastructure, but also, he argues, human interaction was primarily motivated by mutual need.[26] The mutual need White and other scholars who seek to understand Ohio as an in-between locality occupied by social and cultural refugees rests on the assumption of communities of individual actors so thrown out of balance by their disconnect with Eastern peoples that they sought to adopt extralocal cultural ideologies as a form of self-grounding. Understanding Ohio peoples in this way disconnects and fragments our understanding of human action from the possibility of local cultural logics as spatially and temporally continuous.

Getting to the social spaces dictated by the logic of the Longhouse (elaborated in Chapter Two) requires a bit of upstreaming, which is not intended as a way to authenticate or inauthenticate various Iroquois communities outside New York. Rather I am using upstreaming as a way to understand what it was the Sandusky people were doing and what they were doing to be "Sandusky people." I am not ignoring the fact that what they were doing was framed by Iroquois values and sociopolitical practices of the time; rather I am arguing for a recognition of the durability and mobility of the values.

In this way, my approach also engages a form of what Axtell referred to as "downstreaming," where we use the ethnographic literature for clues and as checks on historical documentation.[27] For example, when we read a settler account of a ceremony held at Sandusky in 1820, possessing all of the characteristics of the Iroquois Midwinter as it was documented by ethnographers in the 1950s, it seems appropriate and ethical to refer to the Sandusky ceremony as a "Midwinter." The settlers who were present and wrote about the ceremony named it the "white dog ceremony" or the "burning of the white dog." Yet the ceremony was not simply the burning of a white dog, but instead a multiday communitywide event with multiple intervening socioreligious functions. It also occurred in Midwinter. The Midwinter has changed through time, but continues to help formulate community identity, values, and practices in many contemporary Iroquois communities. In this way, I am using upstreaming, albeit conservatively, as well as downstreaming to focus on social units and values as the source of continuity, and allowing for cultural change and adaptation.

I am also using streaming methodologies to avoid some of the pitfalls presented above which have over time led to the exclusion of the Ohio Iroquois from the "legitimate" world of Iroquois studies. I attempt to present the Sandusky people on their own terms, as represented in the documentation, and up- or downstream as a way of giving context. Thus, mine is not a streaming of cultural inventories for "proof," but rather a streaming of practices for understanding. Sherry B. Ortner tells us about practice, "Whatever the specific purpose of the analysis, however, the general line of questioning is the same: to try and understand something the people did or do or believe, by trying to locate the point of reference in social practice from which the beliefs or actions emerge."[28]

My analytical method 'streams' to prioritize a historical trajectory of community events and interactions with colonial administration rather than an anachronistic sense of time conflating particular meanings across multiple centuries. My concern is with what the historic evidence tells us about a particular moment among a group of people who are by all accounts behaving in ways that make them a cohesive social unit—a cohesive social unit held together by values and practices that provide for a continuity of community. Morris Foster provides a conceptual turn required for recognizing continuity in *Being Comanche*:

> . . . changes in the social conditions surrounding native communities have necessitated changes in the ways in which those communities are constructed; that is, in social relationships and in cultural beliefs and symbols. These changes, however, have been structured along traditional lines that make sense to members of the native communities, not in ways sensible to, or imposed by, members of the Anglo community. In this way, native peoples have continued to construct moral communities within which members' interactions are organized and facilitated.[29]

The construction of the "moral community" at Sandusky further requires an interdisciplinary approach, what I would consider to be a reflection of more recent developments in Native American and Indigenous Studies (NAIS). Under this rubric, knowledge is produced using the methodologies of history, anthropology, literary criticism, social theory, and thinking through forms of local understanding. Therefore, I am not doing history, nor am I doing anthropology, nor am I doing ethnohistory. Rather I am doing a community history and a community analysis. To help, NAIS also attempts to reorient the position from which knowledge is produced. Depending on the subject of study, this approach may be community-directed research or, as in the case of this book, orienting the telling of a social history with an attention to a community's specific use of social units and practices. In this way, I am attempting what Lisa Brooks sets out as a reconstruction of the place-world of a particular group of people through a "place-based" history.[30] Mine is a social history based on what is present, not what is absent, on taking the Sandusky community as they are and as who they are in the documents. It is in fact unabashedly biased toward continuity, but not by claiming that what the Sandusky people were doing in their longhouse was the exact same as what communities in New York were doing in 1950 and had done since time began. No such analytical claims are possible for any community. Rather, the continuity is represented by an interpretation recognizing the Sandusky community as using values to orient social practices, political engagement, and organization through principles having ancient origins in Iroquois culture. The question for this work is how are the Sandusky people behaving as a society, rather than, are they being an Iroquois society? The question of "how" lessens the burden to provide authentication of Iroquoisness, but also allows the Sandusky people to be a community of Iroquois peoples, not a cultural hybrid or a spatial fragment. This simple but significant shift challenges the ideas of Iroquois analytical provincialism and opens the possibility to see social and geographic connections previously discounted in our work.

Shifting to a place-based history at Sandusky requires what Tol Foster suggests: "Instead of looking for some theory to import into indigenous communities, we yield a far more rigorous understanding by both valuing and critiquing the historical and cultural archive as a theoretically sophisticated site of its own. One's history and experience can provide a testable and portable framework for understanding relations between individuals, institutions, and historical forces."[31] To achieve this goal, my reorientation of methodology uses the documentation, such as Indian agent correspondence, trading post records, settler accounts, and U.S. Congressional documents as protoethnographic field descriptions of communal sociopolitical life. As Zhang Xianqing points out, despite the insertion of ethnocentrism and political agendas, protoethnographic accounts should not be discounted, particularly when they contain social practices that can be read from an alternative perspective. These forms of documentation contain "other" histories outside of epistemological and state-derived narratives.[32] Again Tol Foster tells us, what community leaders say and do in the documentation utilizes "counternarratives of their communities as a theoretical base from which to conduct anticolonialist and cosmopolitan critique."[33] Protoethnographic accounts provide the texts through which community and cultural practice is read for the people at Sandusky. The ways people behave through community and cultural practice provide the anticolonial counternarratives to nineteenth-century settlement and contemporary epistemological settlement. This counternarrative of community maintenance and cultural practice, I argue throughout this book, is one of the only reasons the Sandusky people remained a community during the reservation years and were able to continue as a community through the assaults of the late-nineteenth and twentieth centuries.

ONE

PLACE-BASED SANDUSKY HISTORIES

It is well known that the Iroquois made extensive use of the Ohio Territory for hunting and trade before the establishment of villages in the Allegheny drainage and permanent settlement in the Sandusky region. Abounding game and "unclaimed" land made the Ohio Territory an important resource for the colonial economies of Iroquois and Algonquian sociopolitical centers further east. However, not until the late-seventeenth and early-eighteenth centuries was the Ohio Territory inhabited year-round by Iroquois peoples.[1] Overall, scholars see Iroquois migration, and in particular that of the Seneca, as ". . . part of an ongoing expansion since the end of the previous century . . . [and] . . . as a safe haven from problems at home."[2]

Problems at home consisted of increased pressure to cede lands to white settlers and the infiltration of French and British politics into Six Nations politics. Expansion west by the Seneca, for example, also extended Six Nations' political and economic policy by seeking cooperation with nearby tribes as well as attempting to manipulate the British and French through allegiances with groups such as the Delaware and Wyandotte.[3]

Scholarly conceptions of the Iroquois and their relationship to other peoples in the Ohio Territory vary, but tend toward an inherited interpretive provincialism preserving the geographic solidity of the Six Nations. Some see the Ohio Territory as ". . . a volatile land, a prize in a high-stakes game that pitted various British and French interests against Indians trying to preserve their sovereignty."[4] This line of argument tells us the Iroquois, as well as other groups, were attempting to establish their own tribal nation-style governments in the Ohio Territory during the eighteenth century, which were to have been deliberately politically and socially separate from the Six Nations. The Ohio Indian is thought to have sought a sociopolitical identity independent of the Iroquois, fashioned from frontier social relations and recognized by Euro-American governments and regional native populations. Frontier multiculturalism was to have produced native societies based on mutual self-interest. The "multicultural" Ohio Indian population is to have demonstrated their independence from the Confederacy and their European allies by defining "their interests locally" to the extent that foreign and colonial governments were dealing with these communities as individual polities.[5]

Other scholarly interpretations, however, see the "Ohio Country" as a ". . . region the Iroquois [Five Nations] laid claim to on the basis of ancient conquest . . . and the location on it of tribes politically dependent upon them" as evidenced by the Treaty of Fort Stanwix in 1768:

> "The immediate result of the impasse [fighting with the British over trade] was the treaty of Fort Stanwix in 1768, by which the Iroquois surrendered their own and their tribal dependents' claims to the lands south of the Ohio and Susquehanna rivers. The Ohio lands in particular were then used for hunting by, and occupied by villages of Mingo, Shawnee, and other dependents of the Six Nations. The Iroquois, claiming to represent all the occupants and users, negotiated the sale and kept all of the proceeds."[6]

The image of the Ohio peoples as a nationally engaged political entity furthers the notion of a general Ohio Indian with its own hybrid sociopolitical organization under the multiethnic moniker of "Mingo," according to Aquila:

> By 1747, the Five Nations also had to contend with a new political rival. Indians living on the Ohio River and its tributaries were emerging as a power bloc. Pennsylvania officials realized that the Iroquois Confederacy had no control over the Ohio Indians, a conglomeration of individuals from various tribes . . . The Five Nations, fearing that the Ohio Indians would take their place as Pennsylvania's most favored Indian nation moved quickly to prevent a separate alliance between the Pennsylvania government and Ohio tribes.[7]

Trappers, traders, military men, and later settlers used the term *Mingo* as a stand-in for *Indian* to designate the mixed native population moving into and out of the Ohio Valley, which included Iroquois hunters and translocated Shawnee and Delaware. Mingo, or the idea of a multiethnic sociopolitical power block of Ohio Indians, relies on prevailing academic interpretations of ". . . an identity linked to an emerging 'Ohio Indian' world" where Ohio Iroquois along with Algonquians had formed themselves into a socially and politically distinct unit through cross-tribal alliances.[8] These cross-tribal alliances were to have superseded the local, and thus become the basis of the emergence of a sociocultural hybrid acting as a single political unit in its dealings with colonial authority. These cross-tribal alliances, and their assumed multiethnic melding of tradition, however, allow interpretations such as that posited by Downes, who argues that by 1755: "These Indians were gradually reabsorbed into the ranks of their people and thus lost their identity as a factor in the Indian history of the Ohio Valley."[9] The Ohio Indians, through this lens, become significantly culturally detached from the geographic and cultural origins of their heritage, producing the image of native communities uncritically absorbing one another's culture and transforming themselves into something wholly different.

McConnell's interpretation of the Ohio Valley in the eighteenth century challenges multiethnic melding and loss of community identity by supporting a scenario focused on the ways in which autonomy formed intercommunity social and political organization within multiple levels of cooperation and alliance. McConnell proposes a three-tiered level of organization for the Ohio peoples and the Iroquois in Ohio. First, he focuses on a regional identity, the "Ohio Indian," an identity "shared by all inhabitants of the Ohio Country regardless of ethnic affiliation," which would inevitably form the basis of mutual interest for the Western Confederacy of Ohio Territory natives. The larger category of Ohio native contains various "ethnic groups" oriented toward broad cultural affiliations, such as Seneca, Cayuga, Wyandotte, and Shawnee, who seek similar political goals with Euro-American governments. Unlike his predecessors, he further emphasizes autonomous kinship-based towns or villages as the central source of social identity as well as sociopolitical autonomy. McConnell points out: "Although ethnic identities persisted on the plateau [Allegheny], the broad descriptive categories—Shawnee, Delaware, Iroquois—cannot be equated with 'tribes' in any political sense." Instead, Seneca and other Ohio peoples established autonomous towns or villages held together by kinship ties and localism. Towns were organized and founded around a central lineage figure, either a headman or matron. Several multiethnic settlements had been established in the Ohio Valley by the Shawnee, Wyandotte, and Delaware prior to the 1700s, and by the mid- to late 1700s several towns that were identified as ethnically Iroquois had been established within close proximity to the Wyandotte and Delaware in the Sandusky Bay area.[10] The Sandusky Bay as well as the Sandusky River corridor became a geographic homeland for the Wyandotte and Ohio Iroquois peoples.

SANDUSKY LOCALISM

Making any definitive claims about the origins of the Sandusky Iroquois prior to the early 1800s is made difficult by the multiple sources of information coming from French, British, and American interests. Furthermore, settler and military use of general terms such as *Mingo, Seneca,* and *Six Nations* to refer to a variety of natives further complicates the ability to match specific people with specific locales for any length of time. From the late 1600s until the 1750s the Allegheny Valley contained the largest concentration of Western Algonquian and Iroquois settlements. The move into Ohio, according to McConnell, may have been "predicated in part on knowledge of the Ohio Valley. For the Shawnees, firsthand knowledge of the region, its resources and its important stream and trail systems extended back to the late seventeenth century."[11] The Allegheny settlements established by these pioneers, mostly Shawnee, Seneca, and Delaware, were multiethnic trading centers and towns through which more mobile native populations would move, but also served as permanent homes for emerging cooperative communities made up of residential clusters. Residential clusters of people who shared language and culture maintained allegiance to their kin groups and specific kin-based leaders at the same time as they participated in cooperative sociopolitical and economic relationships with others in a village or village complex. Pressures of colonization and settlement on these cooperative villages within western Pennsylvania sparked another westward migration of the Iroquois, Shawnee, and Delaware out of the Allegheny toward the Cuyahoga River Valley in the early 1700s along well-known hunting and war trails extending to Detroit and into French Territory.[12]

The Wyandotte, a group of Huron who moved to Ohio in the 1730s, help us better locate the geographic origins of the Iroquois peoples who would be known as the Sandusky Seneca. The close association of the Ohio Iroquois and Wyandotte began when Iroquois and Algonquian people moved west out of the Allegheny, which coincided with the easterly movement of Huron dissatisfied with their living and trading arrangements with the French in Detroit. The leader of the disaffected Huron was a chief named Angouriot, also known to the French by his baptism name, Nicholas, and to the English as Orontony. Angouriot moved his community from Detroit to the Sandusky Bay in the late 1740s and established the village Etionnontout, located at present-day Castalia, Ohio. The village was also known by the names Ayonoutout and Junundat. Angouriot and his Huron followers became known as "Wendat" by the English; however, I will use Wyandotte, as the community refers to itself today. The village at Etionnontout was a major trade outpost as well as a cooperative community of multiple different native groups including Seneca, Mohegan, Mohawk, and Shawnee. Despite leaving the Detroit area in protest, Angouriot maintained a close trade relationship with the French, who appear to have relied on Angouriot as an eastern ally against the British interests in the area. Despite being considered a "secessionist" for moving away from the Detroit-based Huron, Angouriot received visits from Jesuit priests in 1747 who documented the population of the community at Etionnontout and a nearby settlement they named Aaae. The French Jesuits from Detroit noted the presence of "Six Nations" peoples at the two villages.[13] By 1748 the French had received word that Angouriot and the towns of Etionnontout and Aaae had shifted allegiance to Britain and were planning an attack on Detroit. Angouriot confirmed his break with the French in 1748 when he burned the Huron mission led by Father Pierre-Phillipe Potier on Bois Blanc Island in present-day Ontario, Canada, in retaliation for French militia resistance to his advance on Detroit. He was quite possibly going to the mission to seek allies in his attempt to challenge French domination in the area. However, Father Potier noted the outrage of the Bois Blanc Huron at Angouriot and the "refugee Huron" in a letter to his superior, Father Richardie.[14] After failing to reach Detroit and destroy it, Angouriot returned to Sandusky, burned Etionnontout and fled to Conshake or Konchake (Coshocton, Ohio), where he and a few hundred of his Huron followers lived with other Ohio natives until his death May 20, 1750.[15] The French saw Angouriot's death as ending the Etionnontout "coup," and many of his followers returned to French areas, including Bois Blanc, and others to Etionnontout.[16]

We lose track of Angouriot's people after they migrate back to Sandusky from Conshake or continue west to reunite with the French-allied Huron at Detroit.[17] Angouriot's son Orontondy, however, emerges in the 1770s at Upper Sandusky as an ally to the British against the American rebels. Between the collapse of Etionnontout and the Revolutionary War, the Iroquois in the Sandusky region come into more focus with a mention of the Iroquois village of Canahogue in the Mitchell Map of 1755. The village is documented as across a creek from Angouriot's original settlement. John Mitchell, the author of the map, marked the town of Canahogue on the south shore of Sandusky Bay and noted, "The seat of war, the hart[sic] and Chief Nuntin's grounds of the Six Nations of the lakes of Ohio."[18] Archaeologists David Stothers and Timothy Abel have collected evidence suggesting that Canahogue is the same town as Nunqunhanty and Sunyundeand, which was historically recognized as a multiethnic town consisting of Wyandotte, Delaware, Shawnee, Seneca, and other Iroquois. It is important to note that Nunqunhanty appears on the Bouquet map of 1761 as a multiethnic village of four hundred persons. Nunqunhanty is again thought to have been southeast of the entrance of the Sandusky River into the bay and southeast of Orontony's Etionnontout.[19] From the 1750s through removal, the close association between the Wyandotte and the Ohio Iroquois resurfaces with each community signaling the presence of the other, sometimes with only a brief mention of leaders as signatory on treaties. Throughout the eighteenth and early nineteenth centuries, the documentation bears out a significant political and kin-based allegiance between the two communities; for example, mixed Wyandotte-Seneca emergent leaders during the Revolutionary period, such as Between-the-Logs and Wiping Stick. While not definitive, this close association helps us to come closer to more completely understanding from what early Iroquois groups the Sandusky Seneca emerged.

As the Ohio Territory progresses to the Revolutionary War, the area known as Sandusky at Sandusky Bay on Lake Erie remains a significant British military and trade stronghold in the region, but farther south along the Sandusky River is where the village life of the multiethnic population is centered. The significant British and allied native presence at Sandusky clearly made it a target for Revolutionary as well as French forces and may explain why the communities were concentrated farther south along the Sandusky River. Furthermore, as David Preston points out: "The British army's military colonization of the Ohio Valley, the Euroamerican settlement expansion that followed and intercultural violence were crucial developments in the Ohio Valley in the 1760s. These three legacies of the Seven Years' War would set in motion the fundamental processes shaping Indian-colonist relations in the Ohio Valley for the next fifty years."[20]

Settler violations of the Boundary Line Treaty of 1768 put pressure on communities from the east, while the French put pressure on the largely British-allied Wyandotte and Ohio Iroquois from the west and northwest. Again, we locate the Sandusky region's Iroquois peoples via the Wyandotte. In the 1760s the most prominent town in the region was a village at Upper Sandusky known, because of its association with the Wyandotte leader Tarhe, or Crane, as Crane's Town. Tarhe became a principle figure in the Revolutionary War and treaty signer for the Wyandotte well into the reservation era.[21] By 1770, two villages on the Scioto River, Darby Town and Hell Town, bordering Wyandotte and Delaware settlements, appear as the primary residential areas for the Sandusky-region Iroquois. Moravian Missionary John Heckewelder notes, "there were 2 small Villages of Senecas close upon the Wyondot Villages for many years together one of which the White People (Traders) called Darby's Town and the other Hell Town between the years 1770 and 1780."[22] Hell Town is thought to have been primarily a Delaware and Seneca town founded, along with Darby's Town, in response to continued pressures of settlement after the Six Nations ceded all lands south of the Ohio and Allegheny Rivers to the British without the consent of Ohio Indians in the 1768 Boundary Line Treaty.[23] The move by Ohio Iroquois to Darby's Town and Hell Town may have also been precipitated by the expedition of Lord Dunmore, the governor of Virginia, against "Mingo" and Shawnee settlements on the Scioto River. Dunmore was acting to quell the insurrection of Ohio Indians against settlement of their territory by British colonists.[24] By 1782 Hell Town, which had a sizeable Delaware population, was largely abandoned in response to the March 8, 1782, Gnatenhutten massacre, in which ninety-six converted Delaware were murdered by a colonial American militia from Pennsylvania. At the end of the Revolutionary War and into the nineteenth century, the majority of Seneca were concentrated around Darby Town.[25]

Sparse evidence and brief mention make it difficult to give a highly specific spatial chronology for the Ohio Iroquois, much less the people who would become the Seneca of Sandusky. At best I have been able to assemble evidence of a presence of Iroquois and their participation in multiethnic cooperative villages and political cooperatives. At the same time, the inability to be precise about exactly who was occupying these villages and exactly what is the 'ethnogenesis' of the Sandusky Seneca allows a shift in how we understand the formation of community. In contrast to a concern over the precise 'identity' of the Sandusky Seneca,

I am most interested in the ways in which the Sandusky people were a product of a particular moment in a particular location.

The various forms of native settlements in the Ohio Valley, regardless of their status with colonials and societies of origin, attest to the flexibility of a set of core values to consistently orient Iroquois peoples into communities and kin-based associations from which sociopolitical organizations remained consistent and recognizable across geographic and cultural space. The persistence and use of these values did not go unnoticed by colonial officials, who were very aware of the close relationships between communities at the same time that they recognized differences between groups and their practices. For example, in 1787 it was clear to General Butler, Superintendent for Indian Affairs in the Northern Department, that the Delaware and Wyandotte sought to form a considerable armed resistance to settlement west of the Ohio River boundary established by the British prior to the 1783 Treaty of Paris. Even more explicit are his observations of multiple communities and "nations" as independent actors in relations with one another and with the United States. In contrast to the "mischief" of the Wyandotte and their leader Half King, the well-known Seneca chief Cornplanter had communicated to Butler his desire to remain out of the impending conflict between American forces and Ohio Indians.[26]

British failure to secure the interests of their native allies in the treaty with the United States made the Ohio Indians politically vulnerable as American claims to their lands became more intense. Accordingly, by the Battle of Fallen Timbers in August of 1794, where the Western Confederacy was decisively defeated, the entire Ohio Valley was awash with illegal settlement, violence, kidnapping, and irresolvable tensions between Ohio natives and the United States.[27] Disturbed by the escalations of conflict on the western border, President George Washington directed General Anthony Wayne to form the Legion of the United States, which began its military expedition in 1793 from Fort Washington (Cincinnati, Ohio) and met the Western Confederacy force led by Delaware chief Blue Jacket at the Maumee River. Outnumbered four to one, Blue Jacket's warriors had little chance of victory and were decisively defeated by General Wayne's regiment at a place natives called Fallen Timbers.

The defeat of the Western Confederacy resulted in the cession of the majority of present-day Ohio and Indiana at the Treaty of Greenville in 1795. Attending the treaty conference, Moravian missionary John Heckewelder noted a single Seneca by the name of Reyn-tue-co as a signer.[28] Significant about Reyn-tue-co's presence at the treaty negotia-

tions is the recognition of him as a Seneca, but also as a representative of
a group of Ohio Seneca from "Sandusky" who went against the prevailing desire of the Six Nations Senecas' leadership to avoid conflict with
the United States over the Ohio Territory. Settlers and various government administrators in the Ohio Valley document Seneca participation
in the ongoing debates about the status of the territory, their relations
with surrounding Wyandotte and Delaware peoples, and their continued
contact with the Six Nations. The ten-year period after the end of the
Revolutionary War is seen as a critical moment in the founding of a
multitribal Ohio Indian power block sometimes referred to as the Western Confederacy, but it is also a moment when individual communities
expressed their social, cultural, and individual autonomy.

The Cayuga entered the post-Greenville Ohio Territory in 1807
from the Buffalo Creek Reservation in New York, having recently sold
all of their lands to the United States government. Prior to their migration to the Ohio Territory, the Cayuga became involved in the political affairs of the Ohio Seneca as representatives at the Treaty of Fort
Industry on July 4, 1805: "The Indians residing in Western New York,
having some claim to the land, sent a deputation of not far from thirty
of their number, to attend the treaty at Cleveland."[29] In this treaty the
Wyandotte, Ottawa, Chippewa, Munsee, Delaware, Potawatomi, and
Shawnee Indians relinquished one-half million acres of land south of
Lake Erie and west of the Cuyahoga River in northeastern Ohio. While
the Seneca are not explicitly mentioned, it is likely they were subsumed
under the Wyandotte or Delaware as they had been for previous treaties.

Having already established themselves with the Sandusky people at
meetings during the negotiations leading to the Treaty of Fort Industry,
the Cayuga sold their three small tracts of land in New York in 1807
and began migrating to live with the Sandusky Seneca.[30] After migrating
to the Sandusky region, these Cayuga became identified along with the
Seneca as the "Senecas of Sandusky." John Johnston, who would become
Indian agent at the Piqua Agency, as well as surrounding Anglo settlers
regarded the Seneca and Cayuga as a single community occupying settlements along the Middle Sandusky River and in an area known as Stoney
Creek some forty miles west of Sandusky. What was known by settlers
as "Seneca Town" near present-day Fort Seneca, Seneca County, Ohio,
was the social and political hub for the concentration of the Seneca and
Cayuga populations in the area.[31] There is no documentation concerning
intracommunity distinction about who was Cayuga or Seneca, although
certain community members are sometimes identified by their "nation"
in settler and agent accounts.

Figure 1.1. Sandusky Region Settlements and Reserves. *Source:* Brian J. Gilley and Mary Connors

By 1811 Johnston's agency did the best it could to provide the annuities, supplies, and assistance guaranteed to the signers of the Greenville treaty, but during the fifteen years preceding the War of 1812 it was difficult to keep the natives under his supervision happy while also monitoring British incursions into the area. During the War of 1812, it is presumed that the Senecas on the Sandusky and Stoney Creek remained neutral as they signed an 1814 treaty acknowledging their allegiance to the United States and the prewar property boundaries.[32] Alexander Dallas, Secretary of the Treasury, with duties in the War Department during 1815, explicitly acknowledged continued Sandusky Seneca allegiance to the United States. However, Dallas is unequivocal in his concern over the possibility that the Indians of the "Territory" did not fully understanding that the Treaty of Ghent between the British and the United States was also meant to end hostilities with the native allies of England.

Peace between the Western Indians (primarily the Wyandotte and Shawnee) and the United States was to come at no cost to the natives in terms of land cessions or loss of annuities. In return for agreements to end all hostilities as stipulated in the Greenville treaty, the US would provide redress for past failures to "protect and provide." Additionally, President Madison directed the Western Tribes to "be taught a habit of giving to the public agent constant information of any occurrences that concern the peace and the safety of the Country."[33] Within eighteen months any idea of a slowdown in requests for cession treaties disappeared and John Johnston was directed to begin conversations regarding the establishment of a reserve for each of the Ohio Territory tribes.[34]

In the period leading up to the 1817 Treaty of the Maumee Rapids, John Johnston met repeatedly with the various communities under his agency, attempting to negotiate agreeable terms for land cessions in exchange for defined reservations and increased annuities. Of particular consequence for the Sandusky and Stoney Creek Seneca were attempts by communities of the Six Nations to cede their lands in New York and move to the Ohio Territory to live with their "brethren."[35] Throughout the summer of 1817, numerous councils were held between Indian agents under the Michigan Superintendency and Six Nations tribal leaders. Charles Jouette, Chicago Indian agent, wrote: "The fidelity displayed by these people [the Six Nations] during the recent war, their long habits of intimacy with the whites and the large amount of annuities they receive, being between twenty and thirty thousand dollars, it is thought will furnish a secure guarantee for their good conduct and will interpose a desirable barrier between the other Indians and our frontier settlements."[36] The Six Nations were to be a mediating force between settlers and the Western Indians deemed hostile, such as the Wyandotte, Pottawatomie, Shawnee, and Delaware. The difficulty for the government and the Six Nations was "soliciting a site, which other indians [sic] are ready to grant."[37] However, the Wyandotte, under which the agents included the Seneca and Cayuga living at Sandusky, were unwilling to accept the Six Nations people into their lands and were not willing to be party to a treaty that included them.[38]

The Treaty of Fort Meigs, also known as the Treaty of Maumee Rapids, on September 29, 1817, gave the "Senecas of Sandusky" a thirty-thousand-acre reservation in Seneca County, Ohio, in close proximity to the Sandusky River. Before that treaty was put into effect, another treaty signed on September 17, 1818, enlarged the reserve to forty thousand acres. Reservation life "officially" began on January 4, 1819, when both the 1817 and 1818 treaties were "proclaimed." James Montgomery, a Methodist minister, was assigned as the subagent for the Sandusky Seneca Reservation under the Piqua Agency and the Michigan Superintendency. The Seneca and Cayuga peoples who lived on the Sandusky Reservation occupied a 61.9-square-mile tract in the northern section of the reserve. Because the Cayuga were included among the "Senecas of Sandusky" and were considered Seneca by government officials, they were included in the two five-hundred-dollar annuity payments granted the "Senecas of Sandusky" by the United States in the 1817 and 1818 treaties.[39] The schedule from the 1817 treaty included eighty-three persons all named as the heads of "Senecas of Sandusky" households. In addition to the eighty-three "household heads" were two white captives, William Spicer and Jacob Knisely, known as Crow, who were both married to Seneca women. Therefore taking into account the Wyandotte captive John Vanmeter and his family, who were given a one-thousand-acre tract on the reservation, the total for the population in 1817 was 424 persons. Sometime around 1819, subagent Montgomery reported that there were five groups living within his subagency on the Seneca Reservation. Montgomery reported that there were: ". . . 19 Cayuga families, 157 persons; 9 Seneca families, 64 persons; 9 Oneida families, 48 persons; 6 Mohawk families, 46 persons; 1 Onondagaga family, 7 persons . . . total, 322 persons."[40] By all accounts the Sandusky people, much like their Wyandotte and Shawnee neighbors, combined hunting with small-scale agriculture on one- to two-acre plots. The staple crop was what local settler Isaac Dumond referred to as "soft corn"—also known to botanists as flour corn—which was pounded into meal for cooking and used to create a thick soup. Most of the farming was done by hand with a hoe by women, but toward the end of the reservation era men began to use plows pulled by oxen.[41] The industry of the Sandusky Seneca was noted by Piqua agents, as was their tendency to irrationally cling to "ways of their fathers."

DECOLONIZING FRAGMENTS

Richard White titled chapter 1 of the *Middle Ground*, "Refugees: A World Made of Fragments" and begins: "The Frenchmen who traveled into the pays d'en haut, as they called the lands beyond Huronia, thought they were discovering new worlds. They were, however, doing something more interesting. They were becoming cocreators of a world in the making. The world that had existed before they arrived was no more. It had been shattered. Only fragments remained."[42] In this opening chapter of his now famous argument, White goes on to frame the Ohio Country as a place occupied by indigenous refugees of settlement, colonial imposition, and disease, which were to have produced creative responses among various culturally disparate peoples. The arguments presented here, in this book, do not necessarily challenge White's analysis, because I am convinced that the middle ground was most likely one of multiple intersecting forms of sociopolitical adaptation among the variety of peoples occupying the Ohio Country during a particularly volatile and challenging time period. The middle ground and its general categories of indigenous allegiances no doubt existed parallel to the microsociological entities governed by kinship, language, and shared cultural practice. Also, I am not questioning that colonialism disrupted all facets of indigenous life—communities, economies, cultural transmission, and well-being—challenging the very ability of people to exist. Rather, I question the effect of an analysis framing peoples as refugees and fragments, which goes to the very heart of my criticism of the cultural and historical treatment of Ohio Iroquois peoples in light of Iroquoianist provincialism. Scholars such as Susan Miller criticize White for his erasure of tribal community differences under broad categories, such as Algonquians, and his tendency to artificially disconnect contemporary communities from their Ohio ancestors.[43] I do not disagree with Miller because I see her criticism as reflecting the very thing I am attempting to address albeit from a different angle. The recognition of a general Indian within the *pays d'en haut* and its inability to account for community-level social organization did not begin with White. Rather, it reflects a general disregard for the possibility of communities who chose the Ohio Country as their home and continued to persist in their use of the sociocultural and political practices they brought with them. To name the Seneca and other Iroquois living in the Sandusky region as fragments does not recognize the ways in which these groups of people were in fact continuing to conduct themselves in very Iroquois ways. More importantly, however, is the academic tendency to artificially terminate inquiry into the Ohio peoples in the Revolutionary War era. The best possible explanation one can think of is that if the communities occupying Ohio Country appeared to academics as "fragmented" in their organization, political allegiances, and culture before the Revolution, then after the war and into the reservation era, Ohio Indians are even more difficult to form into cohesive analytical social units. A subtextual reading of "fragment" seems to be a sign for "inauthentic" or so thoroughly "hybridized," the natives in question become homogenized into the category Ohio native, otherwise known as Mingo. The fragment is one disconnected from millennia-old cultural traditions at the moment of their settlement in Ohio in the eighteenth century and during their residence on reservations in the nineteenth century. White's disconnect between the eighteenth-century Mingo of Ohio and the contemporary Seneca-Cayuga pointed out by Miller is simply a natural byproduct of an analytical positioning of the Ohio peoples in a transitional epistemic space. White, it seems, was merely following a long-established academic trend artificially separating Ohio peoples from their cultures of origin. Rather than offering an unnecessary corrective to White and other Ohio "in-betweeners," I seek to provide an intimate portrait as is possible of a single community who were a product of the *pays d'en haut*, as well as other ongoing and parallel sociopolitical, economic, and cultural engagements. This modest goal is inspired by the simple fact that we cannot explain the cultural persistence and sociopolitical continuation of communities such as the Sandusky Seneca into the Seneca-Cayuga of the twenty-first century through an analysis prioritizing "fragmentation."

The goal of my shift in analysis is to puzzle out the ways in which the telling of Iroquois cultural histories follows an epistemological pattern having the effect of endorsing certain cultural patterns while alienating others. This book also tells a story about the ways in which Iroquois studies has dealt with a mixed group of Iroquois—Seneca, Cayuga, Mohawk, Onondaga, and Oneida—who began a geographically mobile orientation in the mid-1700s and found themselves on reservations by 1815. By telling this story I will also tell the early cultural history of the Seneca-Cayuga of Oklahoma, who are the direct descendants of the Seneca of Sandusky as well as the Lewistown Seneca and Shawnee Mixed Band. These stories are intended to begin an overdue conversation about the effects of a unified Iroquois history congealed around highly specific categories of knowledge. With these goals in mind, chapter 2 introduces life at the Sandusky Reservation by explaining cultural continuity and community sustainability through the Midwinter ceremonial. The Midwinter, documented to varying degrees of detail over a ten-year period, provides the scaffolding for "thinking through the Longhouse." "Thinking through the Longhouse" is my way of recognizing the ways in which the community was using local values and practices to orient their social lives. Thinking through the Longhouse is also a way to avoid the ethnohistorical trap of "validation," which seeks to definitively name ceremonies, practices, and other activities or ignore them as inauthentic and unreliable. It is a way of making use of limited documentation without exaggerating or completely ignoring compelling evidence. Thinking through the Longhouse allows us to recognize the ways local cultural logics prevail in the Sandusky people's sociopolitical engagement with the settler state and removal. Chapter 3 examines the community and administrative buildup to removal by offering an interpretation prioritizing community strategies for sociocultural maintenance. In chapter 4 the tragedy, social upheaval, and loss associated with removal is analyzed as an aspect of continual historical mobility rather than simply a narrative for victims of state power. The impact of these analyses, I hope, is to revive the conversation about natives who occupied the Ohio Valley; and in conclusion, I will call on other scholars to extend our understanding of the complexity of the social, political, and economic situatedness natives faced into the nineteenth century.

TWO

Community Maintenance and Midwinter at Sandusky

On November 15, 1831, John McElvain, the Indian agent for the Piqua Agency in Ohio, wrote to Secretary of War Lewis Cass informing him of the impending departure of 340 Seneca and Cayuga the following day from the Sandusky Reservation in Ohio. A few months earlier the "Sandusky Seneca" had signed a treaty for removal to the Neosho Reservation in Indian Territory. Two hundred and thirty Seneca and Cayuga boarded a steamboat while the remainder continued the long and treacherous walk to Indian Territory they had begun two months before.[1]

The removal of the Sandusky people is not unique among tribes who were victims of policies favoring settlers. Neither is their life as removed people in Indian Territory incredibly different from that of numerous other small communities relocated in the first half of the nineteenth century. The time between the late-seventeenth century and the removal of the Sandusky Indians from the Ohio Territory generated numerous sociopolitical adaptations among the Seneca and Cayuga peoples, who made every effort to negotiate entanglements with the French, British, and Americans. While the adaptations may have failed in preventing their continued cession of land and removal, they succeeded in preserving social elements fundamental to community cultural survival.

The brief story of the Sandusky people's removal contains within it a crucial element guiding this book; despite the potential upheaval generated by continued pressure from settlers and the federal government, the Sandusky people left as a community and continue as one today in the Seneca-Cayuga. Rather than an ending to a story about sociopolitical struggle, removal inspires an analysis that seeks to understand the ways in which social institutions were relied upon to ensure the maintenance of a society through its most difficult challenges.

By the time Morgan embarked on his ethnographic historiography of the Iroquois, the Ohio peoples had already translocated to Indian Territory and negotiated a half-century of colonial administration. Their geographic position in the Ohio Territory probably aided their ability to preserve some sense of *communitas* but did not exempt them from being seen by later scholars through multiple epistemological lenses derived from historiographic sedentarianism. The reproduction of stable cultural and spatial characteristics in the epistemological Iroquois is not oriented toward the postcolonial predicament of social, cultural, and physical migration to the frontier away from the 'nation' and away from the 'democratic' locality of the League in the United States proper. The Ohio Territory has long been thought of as a social and geographic fragment of the Iroquois nation; a space disregulated by its lack of a cohesive-seeming cultural orientation. Thus, the ways in which knowledge about the Iroquois is produced, as a set of discursive understandings, have always obtained the potential to endorse and alienate the historiography of multiple fragments. In contrast to localism as a bounded ethnographic or epistemological category, the localism scaffolded by community theories of autonomy becomes a way to stave off the political modernizing projects of the colonial state.

To understand localism as a cultural mechanism derived from community values is to see the ways localism is inherently anticolonial. Localism among the Sandusky people during the reservation era manifests in a refusal to 'nationalize' and thus not allow the modern institutions of nation-state to penetrate their fundamental social institutions. We must, then, avoid the tendency to define nations as communities or communities as nations, which is an analytical problem Kelley and Kaplan tell us produces: "communities of a particularly horizontal kind, intrinsically seeking to live in horizontal symmetries, both internally and externally." The result of horizontal symmetries is analyses unable to think through "post-colonial predicaments," particularly ones conceived of locally rather than nationally.[2]

In this chapter I draw on primary-source material such as letters, firsthand accounts by settlers, Indian agent diaries, and the "as spoken" documentation of the Sandusky people to tell a story about a community that maintained Iroquois social arrangements and had creatively adapted social institutions for engagement with colonial administration. This story centers on the Longhouse, a physical space and a metaphor for the community, and its role as an ideological center for the Sandusky Seneca community.

The Longhouse, the Community

Not much is known about the daily lives of the Sandusky people. Settler accounts, however, provide a portrait of a people not much different from other reservation communities attempting to maintain a semblance of cultural conservatism and autonomy within the continual pressure to cede land and assimilate. What we do know allows us to understand the Sandusky people as a community less distant from their Iroquois roots than previously assumed by scholars and significantly more autonomous in their expressions of a distinct cultural orientation as opposed to the multitribal cooperatives said to predominate among the Ohio peoples. Descriptions of community life, no matter how brief, provide windows into the ways the Sandusky people sought to facilitate the continuation of social institutions by being present to one another and allowing one another to be seen making use of community values in a public setting. As Foster points out, "Public gatherings are vital to community maintenance. They can be used to signal identities in constituent social units of the community and also to hold participants . . . to standards of conduct that emphasize the community they share."[3] Thus, it is the obliviousness of the proto-ethnographic settler to the ways small practices as well as larger communal gatherings function to reinforce the binding fundamental cultural logics where we find the "evidence" of cultural continuity. Settler and Indian agent descriptions of ceremonies, political engagements, brief interactions, and recollections serve, when viewed through an alternative lens, to challenge many of the prevailing assumptions about loss of culture and the erosion of community values. From these bits of history we can draw on the fundamental cultural logics of the Iroquois from their social history to better understand the nature of cultural continuity.

Beyond the brief descriptions provided by settlers, we would have difficulty reconstructing daily life for the Sandusky people, yet it seems we can at least draw a significant understanding of community life from historical documentation of social, ceremonial, and political activities. Any ideas we have about cultural continuity and community on the Sandusky reservation come from the descriptions of the intertwined and overlapping cultural practices, annual ceremonies, and the political organization emanating from them. As practices meant to emphasize the autonomy of community members and the autonomy of the Sandusky people's expressions of cultural logic illustrate the ways in which community life was the result of further cultural commitments rather than remnants of a ruptured social apparatus. In particular, we see continuity between community gatherings, ritual practices, and the ways in which the Sandusky people dealt with the increasing pressures to cede land to the federal government. Understanding the "institutional orders with respect to their inherent possibilities of change"—such as understanding the ways the sport of throwing snow snakes, for example, is integral to the Midwinter ceremony and further linked to the leadership making up administrative embassies used to negotiate treaty arrangements—allows us to see the Sandusky people through their overlapping and autonomous social orientations.[4]

Like their New York Iroquois relatives, the Sandusky people maintained a physical longhouse, referred to as the "council house" by the surrounding nonnative settler observers and government officials. The longhouse functioned to ground the social relations of the Sandusky community by providing the physical basis of the social and political organization; it governed and stabilized expressions of autonomy within the society. The longhouse provides the cultural orthodox with a center for their ceremonial, social, and political interests and activities. Symbolized by the fire left continually burning in its center, the longhouse serves as the central fire of the community literally and figuratively. In general terms, within Iroquois tradition each community is symbolized by its longhouse and each longhouse provides the ontological basis of its congregation. Longhouse communities are jurisdictional entities that derive their authority from the social practices emanating from traditions practiced within the longhouse, such as kinship, political organization, economic exchange, and ceremonies. Longhouses are autonomous social units that share form, function, and belief with other longhouses but are not beholden to the authority of any other congregation. As with any other social unit on the Sandusky Reserve, the Longhouse functioned as a source of individual and community autonomy where the rules of the social community functioned to provide for the people.

The physical and ontological space of the Longhouse produces what I am calling "thinking through the Longhouse" or "the logic of the Longhouse," which is a lens allowing us to think of the Sandusky people's physical space beyond its federal designation as a reservation in the Michigan Superintendency and its people's social life as more than the last-ditch attempt of a defeated people to hang on to mysticism or "revitalize" themselves. Instead we can actively envision a community that drew power, confidence, and continuity from the orthodoxy required by the Longhouse.[5]

The Longhouse is a place of community practice as well as a place for thinking through sociopolitical issues, and in this way it is a lens through which communities view the possibilities and limitations of settlement. The logic of the Longhouse is an analytical tool for recognizing the use of local cultural logics to understand how the members of the community engaged one another socially, but also how local categories framed the ways in which they dealt with colonial administration. It provides for two forms of analytical recognition of the Sandusky people's self-awareness. First, it allows the documentation available to tell the community's story without a comparison to previous academic constructions of an Iroquois culture enshrined in authenticity.

The documents support that many members of the Sandusky Seneca were making extensive use of Iroquois cultural conservative practices, beliefs, and ontology. It is, however, impossible to explicitly name those practices and beliefs according to contemporary or historic categories because neither the Sandusky version nor the Six Nations version is stable or unchanging. The Six Nations version of Iroquois culture is simply better documented than the Ohio in the same way the Six Nations version is trapped by its anthropological history and the other ignored due to its lack of anthropological history. By calling a ceremony documented by settlers the Midwinter, I am not attempting to argue that the Sandusky people were doing the same Midwinter as Iroquois at Six Nations. At the same time, the descriptions of the ceremony observed by settlers follows a pattern academics and Iroquois people alike have come to call Midwinter. The fact that we have trouble naming local categories, and that no one bothered to document what the Sandusky people named them, does not mean that they are not useful for thinking through the community's response to settlement. These logics are rather useful for "thinking with" when doing an analysis of the Sandusky people's social organization. That is, the Longhouse—its rules, categories, principles, and physical presence—is part of a structure of thinking informing the ways communities reproduce themselves over time.[6]

By making analytical use of the Longhouse as a structure of thinking, we find its second use: the logic of the Longhouse allows us to explain how a community maintained its social, political, and religious cohesiveness amidst the varying and aggressive influences of settlement. Too often our analysis of sustained cultural and community persistence ignores that "[natives] may want the freedom to imagine themselves anew, to act in ways that intervene in their destinies, to view themselves as more than the victims of Western dystopias or the happy inhabitants of a communal lark."[7] In this last statement, Craig Womack challenges us to be able to explain native history, literature, orality, values, and behavior, as best as possible, with the potential categories used by natives themselves. Thinking through the Longhouse is my attempt to understand the Longhouse, the Midwinter, and other Sandusky Seneca behaviors through an analytical framework less reliant on congealed ethnoscientific categories requiring methodologies of proof more inherent to the settler than the native. I am simply attempting to take what was observed about the Sandusky Seneca on its own terms and through that process understand how settlement, as well as how we have written about and understood the settled, produces certain forms of knowledge for the studied and student.

The logic of the Longhouse is also a way to recognize the explicit and continual use of a physical longhouse by the Sandusky people as well as its central role in community ceremonial practice. What we know about the longhouse at Sandusky is dependent upon the accounts of settlers and agents, such as Isaac Dumond, who described it circa 1821: "the council-house was built of logs, about 20 feet wide and seventy-five feet long, with three holes in the roof to allow smoke to escape. At these places fires were kept burning. . . ."[8] The original location of the longhouse was on the Sandusky River and sometime before removal the "fire" was transferred to a new longhouse along Green Creek.[9] It was in the Sandusky people's longhouse along Green Creek and around these fires where the community sought to maintain its commitment to cultural conservatism by holding the Green Corn and Midwinter festivals, councils, and treaty negotiations within its walls. It is within this longhouse where the principle political leaders of the Sandusky people gave orations and sought the congregation's continued approval through ceremonial displays of orthodox commitment. Additionally, common among all Iroquois throughout history is the use of the longhouse to extend social relations to other congregations and communities. The Sandusky longhouse served as a way to ensure the interconnectedness of surrounding native groups such as the Wyandotte and Shawnee, who frequently joined them for Green Corn and Midwinter celebrations as well as holding council together to strategize on resisting land cessions in the last days before removal. The Shawnee and Seneca at the Lewistown reservation and the Shawnee at Wapokoneta maintained longhouses of their own with community histories predating the establishment of the Ohio reservations. The relationships among the various "council houses" along the Sandusky did not go unnoticed by settler observers, but they remained confused as to what principles, other than ceremonies and a resistance to "civilization," allowed the interconnections to be maintained.[10] Relations of the longhouse, a center of diplomacy, were also extended to nonnative settlers and Indians agents who were invited to annual festivals, ceremonies, and administrative meetings at the "council house." In this way, the Sandusky longhouse functioned as a physical reminder of the people's spiritual, political, and social autonomy to outsiders. So moved was one settler, Samuel Crowell, by an invitation from the headman Hard Hickory to him and another settler, Obed Dickinson, to a dance at the council house, he showed his affective sympathy for the natives: "And, as in the mind of man there is something intuitive, better known than defined, by which instinctively, as it were, we find in the bosom of another a response to our own feelings."[11]

A range of individuals observed social, religious, and political gatherings at Sandusky among the Seneca community as well as cross-community gatherings with the Wyandotte and the Lewistown Shawnee-Seneca mixed band. The best documentation of social gatherings was that of Methodist missionary James Finley, who recorded his own observations as well as those of other settlers. Finley, who moved with his settler parents to the Ohio Territory at the age of fifteen, provides us with the best descriptions of the Midwinter, councils, and the observations of other settlers. His post as the missionary to the Wyandotte, a church elder for the Sandusky region, and later a subagent for the Piqua Agency required Finley to continually function in the settler and native social worlds.[12] Other settler observers were not regular attendees of social activities, but nonetheless recorded their observations through speeches to community organizations or told their stories to local historians who included descriptions of native lifeways in collected volumes of "recollections." Finley documented his experiences and those of other settlers in his autobiographical *Life Among the Indians* (1859) and *History of the Wyandotte Mission* (1840). William Lang, a Tiffin, Ohio, attorney, collected oral histories and recollections of settler contacts with natives and observations of Sandusky Seneca social practices in his book, *History of Seneca County from the Close of the Revolutionary War to July, 1880*. Settler descriptions from these works as well as other sporadic and brief observations in tertiary sources provide sufficiently detailed accounts of socioreligious activities, such as the Midwinter, for us to, at a minimum, recognize the importance of community participation at the longhouse for the reservation period. Documentation, such as that in Consul Butterfield's 1848 *History of Seneca County: Containing a Detailed Narrative of the Principal Events That Have Occurred Since Its First Settlement Down to the Present Day*, provides vignettes excerpted from unreferenced sources, which make them useful only as descriptive sources. Settler sources seldom provide native perspective on what they were doing and are not detailed enough to document the minutiae of ceremonial activity and change during the period in question. However, in keeping with the goal of this book, I recognize the observations and documentation as possessing the protoethnographic detail allowing a comfortable claim that the Sandusky Seneca were engaged in ongoing sociocultural practices within the traditions of the Longhouse.

Documentation of sociocultural practice, such as the following description of the "Dog Dance" (Midwinter) excerpted from the *Sydney Aurora*, a Shelby County, Ohio, newspaper, and attributed to Piqua subagent Henry Brish for the winter prior to Sandusky Seneca removal, provides a window into Sandusky Longhouse practices.

> We rose early and proceeded directly to the council house, and though we supposed we were early, the Indians were already in advance of us. The first object which arrested our attention, was a pair of the canine species, one of each gender suspended on a cross! One on either side therof. These animals had been recently strangled—not a bone was broken, nor could a distorted hair be seen! They were of beautiful cream color, except a few dark spots on one, naturally, which same spots were put on the other, artificially, by the devotees. The Indians are very partial in the selection of dogs entirely white for this occasion; and for such they will give almost any price. Now for part of the decorations to which I have already alluded; a description of one will suffice for both. First—A scarlet ribbon was tastefully tied just above the nose; and near the eyes another; next round the neck was a white ribbon, to which was attached some bulbous, concealed in another white ribbon; this was placed directly under the right ear, and I suppose it was intended as an amulet or charm. Then ribbons were bound round the forelegs, at the knees and near the feet—these were red and white alternately. Round the body was a profuse decoration—then the hind legs were decorated as the fore ones. Thus were the victims prepared

and thus ornamented for burnt offering. While minutely making this examination, I was almost unconscious of the collection of a large number of Indians who were there assembled to offer their sacrifices. Adjacent to the cross was a large fire built on a few logs; and though the snow was several inches deep, they had prepared a sufficient quantity of combustible material, removed the snow from the logs and placed thereon their fire. I have often regretted that I did not see them light this pile. My own opinion is, they did not use the fire from their council house; because I think they would have considered that as common, and as this was intended to be a holy service, they, no doubt, for this purpose struck fire from a flint, this being deemed sacred.

It was clear, beautiful morning, and just as the first rays of the sun were seen in the tops of the towering forest and its reflections from the snowy surface, the Indians simultaneously formed a semicircle enclosing the cross, each flank resting on the aforesaid pile of logs.

Good Hunter, who officiated as High Priest, now appeared, and approached the cross; arrayed in his pontifical robes, he looked quite respectable. The Indians being all assembled—I say Indians, for there was not a squaw present during all this ceremony—at a private signal given by the High Priest, two young chiefs sprang upon the cross and each taking off one of the victims, brought it down and presented it on his arms to the High Priest, who receiving it with great reverence, in like manner advanced to the fire, and with a very grave and solemn air, laid it thereon—and this he did with the other—but to which, whether male or female, he gave the preference I did not learn. This done, he retired to the cross.

In a devout manner he now commenced an oration. The tone of his voice was audible and somewhat chanting. At every pause in his discourse, he took from a white cloth he held in his left hand, a portion of dried, odoriferous herb, which he threw on the fire; this was intended as incense. In the meanwhile his auditory, their eyes on the ground, with grave aspect and solemn silence, stood motionless, listening attentively to every word he uttered.

Thus he proceeded until the victims were entirely consumed and the incense exhausted, when he concluded his service; the oblation now made and the wrath of the Great Spirit, as they believed, appeased, they again assembled in the council-house, for the purpose of performing a part in their festival, different from any I yet had witnessed. Each Indian as he entered, seated himself on the floor, thus forming a large circle; when one of the old chiefs rose and with that native dignity which some Indians possess in a great degree, recounted his exploits as a warrior; told in how many fights he had been the victor; the number of scalps he had taken from his enemies; and what at the head of his braves, he yet intended to do at the "Rocky Mountains;" accompanying his narration with energy, warmth and strong gesticulation; when he ended, he received the unanimous applause of the assembled tribe.

This meed of praise was awarded to the chief by "three times three" articulations, which were properly neither nasal, oral nor guttural, but rather abdominal. Thus many others in the circle, old and young, rose in order, and proforma, delivered themselves of a speech. Among those was Good Hunter; but he "Had laid his robes away His mitre and his vest."

His remarks were not filled with such bombast as some others; but brief, modest and appropriate; in fine, they were such as became a priest of one of the lost ten tribes of Israel. After all had spoken who wished to speak, the floor was cleared and the dance renewed, in which Indian and squaw united, with their wonted hilarity and zeal.

Just as this dance ended, an Indian boy ran to me and with fear strongly depicted in his countenance, caught me by the arm and drew me to the door, pointing with his other hand towards something he wished me to observe.

I looked in that direction, and saw the appearance of an Indian running at full speed to the council-house; in an instant he was in the house and literally in the fire, which he took in his hands and threw fire, coals and hot ashes in various directions through the house and apparently all over himself. At his entrance, the young Indians much alarmed, had all fled to the further end of the house, where they remained crowded, in great dread of this personification of the Evil Spirit. After diverting himself with the fire a few moments at the expense of the young ones, to their no small joy he disappeared. This was an Indian disguised with a hideous false face, having horns on his head, and his hands and feet protected from the effects of the fire.

And though not a professed "Fire King," he certainly performed his part to admiration.

During the continuance of this festival, the hospitality of the Senecas was unbounded. In the council-house and at the residence of Tall Chief, were a number of large fat bucks and hogs hanging up and neatly dressed.

Bread, also, of both corn and wheat, in great abundance. Large kettles of soup ready prepared, in which maple sugar, profusely added, made a prominent ingredient thus forming a very agreeable saccharine coalescence. All were invited and made welcome; indeed, a refusal to partake of their bounty, was deemed disrespectful, if not unfriendly.

I left them in the afternoon enjoying themselves to the fullest extent, and so far as I could perceive, their pleasure was without alloy. They were eating and drinking, but on this occasion, no ardent spirits were permitted—dancing and rejoicing—caring and probably thinking not of to-morrow.[13]

As a description of community practice the text locates the ways of the Longhouse at the core of Sandusky Seneca social life. In keeping with the goal of the analysis we also find in the description clues about the ways community dispositions coalesced around socioreligious practices with origins in the Great Law of Peace and its attendant principles. This and other narratives or recollections of the "Dog Dance" pose a significant challenge to any interpretations favoring a fragmented or hybrid view of Sandusky Seneca social life. More than simply providing the details required to know that what the settlers called the "Dog Dance" was actually the Midwinter, the descriptions of the ceremony indicate a certain commitment to cultural conservatism. In Sandusky cultural conservatism, when read through a theoretical apparatus prioritizing autonomy, we also see a community behaving in ways solidifying a communal cohesiveness and solidarity. Cohesiveness and solidarity would be required in the social apparatuses necessary to hold the Midwinter during the reservation period and would have required a strong orientation toward Iroquois traditionalism as well as significant support from a large number of community members. To hold a Midwinter would require the knowledge to conduct the ceremony in the proper way as well as the commitment of significant human and material resources. Hosting and seeing through such a ceremony is no small act and thus tells us about the social units and practices held as important among the community.

The socioreligious pressures on the Sandusky people from settlers also reveal their consistent support of Longhouse principles as well as their commitment to autonomy. The stories about Between-the-Logs, who was an influential Christian convert and leader of the Bear clan among the Wyandotte, give us some detail about the social atmosphere among the Sandusky people.[14] Between-the-Logs, only briefly a follower of the Code of Handsome Lake, converted to Methodism in his mid-twenties and was seen by missionaries as a perfect mediator for evangelizing among the Wyandotte and his father's people, the Sandusky Seneca, with whom, and with whose longhouse, Between-the-Logs had regular contact. James Finley, the minister in charge of the Methodist mission to the Wyandotte, was crucial in Between-the-Logs' conversion and became his mentor in evangelical pursuits. Another converted Wyandotte, Mononcue, also traveled with Between-the-Logs and other Methodist ministers around Ohio, Pennsylvania, and New York, evangelizing to natives, fundraising for missions, and attending Methodist conferences.[15]

James Finley's narrative of a trip to the Sandusky Seneca community in July of 1823 with Between-the-Logs, Mononcue, and other ministers provides a portrait of the influence of the Code and Christianity among the Sandusky Seneca as well as local recognition of the Seneca as practitioners of their "ancient religion." On an 1823 mission trip, Finley, Mononcue, and Between-the-Logs were traveling through the Sandusky area speaking at community gatherings and spreading "the word." They had come to what Finley identified as a Mohawk town, but they were told everyone had gone to the Seneca council house at Sandusky for a feast. Soon after their arrival at the council house, the headmen presiding over the gathering passed the pipe and welcomed the visitors: "We are happy to inform you that the Great Spirit has appointed four angels to take care of our nation; and that our old prophet (meaning the far-famed Seneca prophet) does not forget to visit us once in a while, and tell us what to do. He was seen by one of our young men the other day, and he told him we must hold our great feast for him, which we have done these last four days."[16]

The appearance of Handsome Lake's spirit so disturbed Between-the-Logs that he fell to his knees and began singing a Methodist hymn, in which Mononcue and Finley joined in praise. Some ceremonial attendees left the longhouse outraged by the sudden display of Christian worship. The chief presiding over the ceremony, however, welcomed Between-the-Logs and encouraged him and the other converts to speak their mind, to which they responded with speeches admonishing the community for "heathen" practices. John Pointer, the interpreter who accompanied the missionary group, translated segments of the speeches from Seneca to English and Finley recorded them in his journal. Between-the-Logs addressed the congregation: "We thought that as our business was from the Lord, we would come on his day . . . on which to worship him. We expected to find you at your homes, or in some good employment, on this day of rest; but we were disappointed, for we found many of you playing ball." He continued: "Such was the late revelation concerning the four angels to take care of your nation, and the appearance of your Seneca prophet. This is all guess work, and is not to be trusted; for you and I both know that it is all in the dark."[17]

Another Wyandotte convert, Hicks, arose to speak: "Brothers, I am this day confused and astonished. I think you ought to have treated us with more respect; for when you came to our town with your old prophet, we sat down and heard all you and he had to say with patience. Some of our people believed him, and joined him."[18] Mononcue then rose, attempting to settle the resistance that was building among the congregates: "When you meet to worship God and to hear from his word, shut up your mouths, and open your ears to hear what is said. You have been here several days and nights, worshiping your Indian god, who has no existence, only in your dark and beclouded minds. You have been burning your dogs and venison for him to smell. What kind of god or spirit is he, that can be delighted with the smell of a burnt dog? Do you suppose the great God that spread out the heavens . . . is pleased with the smell of your burnt dogs? I tell you to-day, that his great eye is on your hearts, and not on your fires, to see and smell what you are burning."

A headman rose in response to the speeches: "We all speak one word—that is, we all believe in our old Indian religion. But we will hold a council on your words, and call you again to this place to hear our reply." Between-the-Logs stayed behind at the council house for the duration of the ceremony, during which several Seneca were to have told him that only the chiefs "speak with one mind" and that many members of the community were in fact Christian.[19]

Finley's entire recounting of the day he spent at the Sandusky longhouse, and the souls he was to have saved, not surprisingly favor the settler and Christianity. Alternatively, the degree of disgust and astonishment among the evangelizers can also be read as signaling a degree of cultural conservative commitment on behalf of the community. Finley's recounting of the interaction at the council house tells of a community, or at least part of a community, responding to a young man's dream of the Prophet through Iroquois ceremonialism and community commitment to certain Longhouse principles. The missionaries' admonishment of the Sandusky Seneca for their lack of Christianity also signals a noteworthy degree of local commitment to ceremonialism.

Settlers' Christian sympathy and disgust toward the local natives did little to reconcile their misunderstanding of the ways certain fundamental principles organized all community life at the longhouse. At Sandusky the ontological realities of community life were an extension of the values, ethics, and morals of the Longhouse. Community life included multiple opportunities for Sandusky people to access the Longhouse principles and express individual and lineage autonomy. For example, what settler observers referred to as "the ball game" (lacrosse) was a common activity in the summer. Lacrosse, according to Iroquois cultural conservatives, is "the Creator's game," as it is designed to please and appease the Creator. Lacrosse was also a way for warriors to keep fit and for young aspiring warriors to acquire confidence and dexterity. Historically, lacrosse functioned as a way to alleviate sociopolitical tensions within or between villages or factions. Lacrosse was a way to extend social relations between broader regional groupings, such as maintaining political allegiances between the Seneca and Mohawk, for example, but also functioned to reaffirm clan ties across various microsociological levels of social organization. Typically, lacrosse was organized into teams according to moiety and clan affiliation. These affiliations provided the ability to draw team members from other villages and communities when larger, multicommunity events were held. Lacrosse also became an important aspect of treaty negotiations, during or after which tension or celebration would precipitate a game.

The Sandusky observed the "ball game" as a community practice, and it is in the settler descriptions from the 1820s where we find evidence of the continued use of the clan and moiety system to organize the game. Protoethnography by settlers also describes events where community members turned out to support their relatives with cheers of encouragement, wagering, and ample food. Glimpsed through simple observations by settlers describing secular sporting traditions or deploring the "idle" frittering of precious time, lacrosse provides us with a deeper understanding of the ways the Sandusky people continued to organize themselves within ancient principles.[20]

The ball game is but one of the multiple interconnected social practices where the Sandusky people likely maintained their fundamental social institutions ("the inside") where the logic of the Longhouse oriented all sociopolitical activity. As a reflection of "the inside"—the practices whose internal logic is the least discernible by the colonizer and the least useful for nationalist projects—the ball game reflects the logic of the Longhouse, which reflects the Sandusky people's desire to maintain respectful relations to one another, but also to the spirit beings who help guide social and political organization.

Understanding the ball game as one of many autonomous and undifferentiated institutional elements allows us to conceive of community life as perpetuated through the cultural logics providing the socio-cultural foundation of the Sandusky people. The Sandusky people were what Champagne calls "cultural conservatives," where the "worldview expressed in Indian religions is included within the undifferentiated cultural elements and serves to reinforce the undifferentiated relations among art, morality, ceremony, religion and causality."[21] An analysis seeing community life through the lens of the Longhouse—as an expression of undifferentiated institutional relations—provides a view of Sandusky community life as something providing for cultural continuity. In this analysis cultural continuity is not forced onto a historical documentation. Rather, cultural continuity emerges as the maintenance of community life through deliberate change, not change solely in reaction to colonial oppression and the gradual assimilation of social elements.

FOURTEEN SANDUSKY MIDWINTERS

During the Sandusky period the Seneca and Cayuga peoples living on the reservation maintained community and individual commitment to the Midwinter ceremonial but also to the ways in which the ceremonial was integrally linked to the community's attempt to protect political and social autonomy. The Midwinter celebration, called the Dog Dance by settlers because two white dogs are ritually sacrificed and burned on the last day, was the most significant ceremonial practice among the Sandusky people. Over the fifteen-year period of reservation life, 1817–1831, the Midwinter took place at the Sandusky longhouse and included a significant number of local nonnatives as well as neighboring communities of Wyandotte and Shawnee.[22] As a center of communal life, the Midwinter provided the socioreligious orientation for the maintenance of undifferentiated social elements crucial for the continuation of fundamental cultural logics—cultural logics we will see extended to the community response to political necessities brought on by colonial administration. Thus, the ceremony provides the opportunity to reify, modify, and preserve the fundamental principles running through all communal and individual action. The community's autonomy did not go unnoticed by the Indian agents, missionaries, and local settlers who noted the frequency with which the natives held council and ceremonies and resisted settler culture. Settlers also clearly understood the nonsecular nature of the communities' activities as well as the religious basis for a community leader's authority. Whether intended to or not, the continued open practice of Iroquoian ceremonialism and the public participation of Sandusky Seneca leadership in ceremonies served as a reminder of native resistance to settlement for the local nonnatives and government authorities, who recognized the community as "adhering to the customs of their forefathers."[23]

By accepting the Sandusky people as organized within the values of the Longhouse as well as recognizing the values of the Longhouse as prizing low societal differentiation, we can see the Midwinter ceremony as a central aspect in the maintenance of social life documented at the Sandusky longhouse. Within the ritual context of the Midwinter, a community-specific intentionality prevails through continual displays of individual, collective, and cosmic autonomy as well as the recognition of the power of the practices within institutions that scaffold cultural continuity. Again, in the Midwinter, as Champagne points out, "the content . . . of the undifferentiated structural relations among cultural elements combine and interpenetrate to foster conservative orientations."[24] The Midwinter, as a conservative social practice, is one of many forms of interpenetrating cultural elements that sought to reinforce an adherence to the fundamental logics of the Longhouse. The Midwinter ceremony, known as *Gänä`yasta`* in Seneca, was designed within the logic of the Great Law to address societal concerns by maintaining good relations between humankind and other autonomous beings of the world. Crucial for good relations is the offering of thanks to agricultural produce (corn, beans, and squash), the Sun, the Moon, and the Thunderers. Midwinter was also an opportunity to celebrate with deceased relatives who return to dance with the living and cure the sick. Tobacco invocations, dances, games, feasting, prayer, and orations, referred to as "doings" by many cultural conservatives in the mid-twentieth century, were woven throughout the Midwinter ceremony and acted to reinforce a life lived according to the principles of the Longhouse. Principles of the Sandusky longhouse may have included the teachings of Handsome Lake, who visited Sandusky in the early 1800s. However, the influence of the

Code's theological revisions are not obvious in settler descriptions of the Sandusky Midwinter despite some of the activities described falling into general directives for worship by Handsome Lake. Some possible indicators of Handsome Lake's influence are the preaching of abstinence from alcohol during the actual ceremony and the prominent role the Creator (or God) takes in ritual and celebration. Settler accounts, however, do not provide a level of detail or narration allowing a definitive claim for the presence of the Code.[25]

Gänä`yasta` at Sandusky is documented as being "around Christmas," as well as late winter or early spring. The Sandusky community prepared for the ceremony by hunting enough game to feed a few hundred participants over several days. The men traveling and hunting along the Sandusky River also announced the date and place of the Ceremony to surrounding natives and friendly settlers. Once the date was set, "And in crowds the Indians now came into Lower Sandusky, with their venison and their skins, and the squaws with their painted baskets and moccasins, not . . . to barter for necessaries, but chiefly for ornaments."[26] In the days immediately preceding the ceremony, community members began preparing themselves for the oncoming intensity of interaction by holding snow-snake-throwing competitions, lacrosse games, and the sacred bowl games. Two white dogs were chosen for sacrifice, which "were selected months in advance, well fed and made fat. They were as near alike as possible and with yellow spots."[27] Prior to the ceremony, two men known as Big Heads went to community members' houses and "stirred the ashes" of family fires, revitalized the fires at the longhouse, and delegated preparatory work such as maintaining fires, cleaning the longhouse, gathering wood, and guarding ceremonial objects to other community members. After the Big Heads had circulated through the houses, a series of shots were fired to signal the beginning of the ceremony and to call everyone to the longhouse.[28]

The ceremony at Sandusky began with a thanksgiving speech by a headman of authority who was chosen to speak for the community. The thanksgiving speech set the tone for the ceremony and outlined the issues of community and individual concern to be addressed by "the doings." As documented by settlers, Sandusky headmen Good Hunter, Hard Hickory, and Tall Chief were the primary speech-makers at the Sandusky longhouse during the reservation era and, as we see in chapters 3 and 4, were also the primary negotiators of the treaties for removal. Good Hunter is described as a "full-blood Seneca" having a "melancholy look . . . a little gray" and "about fifty years old" in 1832. Hard Hickory "was a large, noble looking man, and nearly half white, about six feet high, had little chin whiskers, was very straight and muscular, spoke English well and was highly respected." He too was in his fifties in the early 1830s. Tall Chief is described even more sparsely as "a tall, noble looking specimen of an Indian, sober and honorable."[29] In their speeches these men thanked the other beings with whom they shared earth and community and thanked "the Prophet" and the Creator. Through their thanksgiving to other beings and spirits, the men would emphasize many of the values they sought to maintain and protect by interweaving their knowledge of community history, Iroquois oral tradition, and current challenges faced by the people. For seven days the Midwinter would continue to give thanks to people and spirits through orations, ceremony, and feasting. Interwoven into the thanks were a series of dances to honor war feats, dream interpretation, healing rituals, and recognition of the spirits of False Face societies.

In the Sandusky Midwinter longhouse men and women danced and worshiped in their best "Indian clothes" with silver hair plates, medallions, silks, brass bells, and beaded clothing. They danced to a central drum fashioned between two wooden poles, water drums made of hide and wooden kegs, and rattles made of gourds or turtle shells. Samuel Crowell observed: "At the commencement of each dance a chief rose and began to sing with slow sonorous and strong syllabic emphasis keeping time with his feet and advancing round the house, directly rose another, one after another, rising and singing the same word. Next the squaws, by seniority, rose and united in the song and dance." During the dance, weapons were fired into the air signaling the beginning and ending of each portion of the day's ceremony. Throughout the ceremony participants were fed from central kettles of game meats and squash. Many of the settler observers were invited to participate in the dancing, feasting, and ritual and to take overnight accommodations in community homes and the actual longhouse.[30]

The Midwinter of 1831 was the last stirring of the ashes at Sandusky. The Seneca had agreed to cede their lands, and community leaders would be traveling to Washington, D.C., in February to finalize the treaty. The Sandusky Seneca would move to Indian Territory the coming fall. As a ceremony setting the tone for the spring and the possibilities the season holds, the last Gänä`yasta` in Ohio no doubt held even greater significance, particularly for the men representing the community at treaty negotiations and charged with the removal of their own people. Samuel Crowell, a local settler, stayed at Hard Hickory's home on the last night of the 1831 Midwinter. Hard Hickory told him of a dream which required him "to appease the anger of the Good Spirit":

> He dreamed he was fleeing from an enemy; it was he supposed, something supernatural—perhaps an evil spirit; that after it had pursued him a long time and for a great distance, and every effort to escape from it seemed impossible, as it was now at his heels, and he almost exhausted. At his perilous time he saw a large water, to which he made with all his remaining strength, and at the very instant, when he expected every bound to be his last, he beheld to his joy, a canoe near the shore; this appeared as his last hope; breathless, and faint, he threw himself into it, and that moment, of its own accord, quick as an arrow from the bow, it shot from the shore, leaving his pursuer behind.[31]

After dictating Hard Hickory's dream, Crowell reveals:

> While relating this circumstance to me, which he did with earnestness, trepidation and alarm strongly expressed in his countenance, he took from his bosom something neatly and carefully enclosed in several distinct folds of buckskin. This he began to unroll, laying each piece by itself, and on opening the last there was enclosed therein a miniature canoe. On handing it to me to look at . . . that as a memento, he would wear it in his bosom as long as he lived.[32]

Hard Hickory's desire to see the contents of his dream resolved with the Creator was a crucial aspect of the Midwinter known as the Dream Guessing ritual. Dream Guessing was a multiday activity where individuals would present their dreams for interpretation by the community. It involved revealing small clues from a dream while the community guessed at its contents and did what they could to relieve the anxiety caused by the dream. Dream Guessing also included the interpretation of dreams seen as more sacred for their potential to reveal purpose, danger, and instructions for the dreamer. Hard Hickory no doubt thought he had experienced one of these sacred dreams because he had constructed or had been given a miniature canoe as a form of protective medicine.[33] Given that the community was about to embark on an important journey and Hard Hickory's significant role in negotiating the terms of their removal, it is not surprising he sought to ensure the recurrence of the dream in sleep and in life through the dream renewal and fulfillment aspect of Dream Guessing. As protective medicine, the miniature canoe was no doubt intended to ensure his continued success in escaping enemies, in cleverness and luck in dangerous situations, and in the maintenance of good relations with the Creator.[34] Dream Guessing in the Midwinter expresses the logic of the Longhouse by allowing community members to fulfill one another's dreams and provide supernatural support for good and bad dreams. The cooperative support of one another's dreams articulates with thanksgiving in the Midwinter and provides what Father LeJeune observed at Dream Guessings in the 1650s as the "prop and maintenance of their whole State."[35] Dream Guessing is but one of the interacting elements of the ontological foundation of the Sandusky longhouse which connects the autonomous spirit beings of the Iroquois world. The sacrifice of the white dogs is said to fulfill the dreams of the Creator and follows multiple days of Dream Guessing.

After the sacrificed dogs were burned, Good Hunter began the tobacco invocation. The solemn and reverent congregation listened and quietly absorbed the words of Good Hunter until the dogs had been entirely consumed by the fire. Following the tobacco invocation, the men of Sandusky began the Rite of Personal Chant, in which men would sing songs given to them by their families and recount their war exploits. Following the chants, the dancing of the various medicine societies resumed, only to be interrupted by the appearance of a member of the False Face Society who entered the longhouse wearing a mask, jumped into the fire, threw ashes about, and wiped them on his body. After the False Face was appeased with tobacco, the dancing resumed and the last day of feasting began.[36]

Midwinter Subjectivities

The fourteen years of Midwinter is not simply an indicator of a certain degree of "traditionalism." It is more of a reflection of a sociocultural and political orientation for the Sandusky people, which becomes reflected in the various forms of subjectivity created through the logic of the Longhouse. Subjectivities are produced by the use of the longhouse as a physical space, its metaphysical maintenance through "the doings," and the knowledge required to conduct community social and religious business within its actual and metaphorical walls. The logic of the Longhouse produces a set of physical and esoteric orientations held together by principles prizing the interpenetration of social elements. Recognizing the ability of the logic of the Longhouse to inform sociohistorical events and practices also challenges the epistemological construction of Sandusky Iroquois as fragments or products of hybrid social institutions. The longhouses whose fires would become the fire of the Sandusky longhouse, the Midwinter, and all the social, material, and ceremonial relations required to maintain a longhouse challenge the idea of an in-between.

Returning to the fundamental arguments of this book, the Midwinter serves as a lens through which to connect various forms of continuity between political organization, sociocultural practices, and the persistence of community values. For example, even though we do not have detailed descriptions of kinship patterns among the Sandusky people, for the Midwinter to exist, kinship would have had to ground the extensive inter- and intracommunity affinities crossing tribal, language, and cultural boundaries as well as provide some understanding of the nonnatives progressively encroaching on all sides. Observing these relations as belonging to groups of individuals and communities seeking different forms of consensus, organization, and continuity through recognition of one another's autonomy is a natural extension of the mere existence of rituals such as the Midwinter. Making this connection requires downstreaming, upstreaming, and a certain amount of faith in the evidence. However, in lives viewed through the longhouses of the Sandusky people and their neighbors, we see the power of the "council house" to organize the people, their desires, and their challenges through the most durable cultural logics of the Iroquois. When the use of the physical space of the Longhouse is connected to the social practices organized according to Longhouse principles, we see, for the first time as scholars, in the Sandusky people a set of dispositions functioning to ensure the maintenance of community life. Thus, practices such as the "ball game," or lacrosse, extend the arrangements of the Longhouse to the playing field and thus reinforce the conceptual footing upon which the Longhouse stands.

The Midwinter further evidences the potential for a different understanding of the political and social challenges faced by the Sandusky community. In the next chapters we see the logic of the Longhouse and the subjectivities it produces shaping the ways in which the community and its leaders negotiated the sociopolitical terrain of settlement pressures and the demands of colonial administration. The political organization, with the Longhouse as its scaffold, and with which the Sandusky people engaged the pressure of settlement, provides a further testament to ways in which they sought to represent themselves through community cultural logics and in clear-minded council with each other and the Creator.

THREE

REPRESENTATION AND AUTONOMY

No one can be more desirous of seeing our Indians all settled west of
the Mississippi than I am. They cannot be preserved long on what is
called Reservations in this country, but they cannot be forced. They
will gradually move themselves as our population crowds on them. . . .

—John Johnston to J. C. Calhoun, in 1824

In the months after the last Midwinter ceremony, community leaders at
Sandusky finalized the arrangements for their removal at a meeting in
Washington, D.C. However, the pressure to remove began fourteen years
before, in 1817, almost immediately after the signing of the Treaty at
the Foot of Maumee Rapids, which established the Sandusky Reservation. Interaction with the United States government and white settlers
became increasingly more frequent during the reservation period. Of
primary concern and the cause of much frustration for the Sandusky
peoples was settler encroachment on their lands and the influence of
Euro-Americans on their society. In a council between officials from
the federal government and community representatives on February 19,
1824, a translator recorded the following statement from the "Seneca
Chiefs":

You know that this country was once ours. It is true we have
sold it though contrary to our wishes. We have now but a small
tract of Land on which we want to live and die . . . But our
hearts are often made sick. Whiteman passing through our Land
often say this land is to [sic] good for Indians—We fear that we
will soon be driven from this cuntry [sic] unless you help us.[1]

Settlers in the Ohio Territory obtained their land primarily by squatting and purchasing former Indian property from the government. In 1821 the government conducted a sale of the Ohio peoples' lands taken in the 1817 treaty. Shortly after the Sandusky peoples moved to the reservation, their homes and fields on the west side of the Sandusky River were appropriated by white settlers. By 1823 a town and a populous settlement were growing up around the Sandusky Reservation to the east. The settlers had constructed a mill, formed a militia, and developed a considerable trade with the southern portion of Ohio.[2] The pressure of settlement increased exponentially every year for all Native peoples occupying Ohio. As early as 1817, even before the Seneca and others began residing on the Sandusky Reservation, removal was being discussed among Indian agents, the president, and other federal agencies.[3]

The ongoing communications between the Sandusky people, Indian agents, Congress, and the president show a community which sought to preserve its way of life and sociopolitical autonomy. Letters, recorded orations, and details of discussions also tell us about a community that had yet to adopt a governmental structure mirroring that of its imperial overseers, which makes the logic of the Longhouse critical for understanding how the Sandusky people engaged the political-economic demands of the U.S. federal system. As historian Mark Rifkin points out, representation and negotiation are normalized where "the administratively orchestrated consent of internalized populations can serve as a means of validating U.S. legal geography by presenting its terms as the self-evident terrain on which negotiation occurs."[4]

In this chapter I offer an additional critical understanding to the "self-evident terrain" by pursuing a discussion of the ways in which the logic of the Longhouse served as the fundamental basis of political engagement. While the federal government representatives were using an "administratively orchestrated consent," the Sandusky people were guided by community principles. Seeing the Sandusky people's efforts to negotiate removal pressure through the administrative logic of the federal system, we see only fragmented and disorganized attempts to avoid cession and relocation—the failed attempts of a people weakened by their lack of state-styled government. Applying a community-inspired analysis, however, shows a form of political engagement emanating from the same cultural logics dictating other societal institutions, such as the Midwinter, and thus the probability of a continued commitment to decentralized leadership and low societal differentiation among cultural elements.[5] The removal of the Sandusky people might be seen as their failure to effectively and powerfully negotiate with the federal government. Alternatively, removing on their own terms, as a community of autonomous beings, might have been of much greater importance than avoiding removal altogether.

REPRESENTATION AND REMOVAL

Analytical dependence on notions of transience, fragmentation, and refuge relies on settler society's habit of "constituting communities through specifically imperial institutions of representation which lie in contrast to the local institutions of representation."[6] Representation is both the settler's image of the Ohio Indian, and the settler state's formalized modes of political authority, accountability, and constituent delegation. The imperial institutions of representation most commonly found in the nineteenth-century Ohio Valley were semiotic as it produced the image of the "difficult" Native who was resistant to change, without reason, and insolent to Manifest Destiny. Settler representations of Ohio Indians generated an image that converged on the political process surrounding land cession, where delegations from both sides met as representatives of their respective constituencies. The federal Indian bureaucracy, inspired by its own habits of documenting representations of Natives and politically representing for Natives, sought to consolidate Indian community representation in a few individuals who were willing to sit down and hammer out suitable agreements. Federal institutions expected to deal with consistent leadership and demands from Ohio peoples. However, the decentralized political system of the Sandusky people was read through the image of "the difficult Indian," which furthered frustration of the Indian agents and bureaucrats assigned to pursue the swap of Ohio lands for a reservation in Indian Territory. The Sandusky community constructed in the minds of the agents, settlers, and later, scholars, was disorganized with unreliable and indecisive leadership evidenced by the variable representation at negotiations, fluctuating demands, and Indian unwillingness to make a "timely" decision. Scholars later interpreted these variabilities as a political system guided by self-interested chiefs, wrought with factionalism, infighting, and intertribal rivalries. Reorienting the sign "Ohio Indian" and its analytical effects requires recognition of local conceptions of political agency and social continuity.[7]

My concern in this chapter is with the ways the representational habits of the colonizer have come to frame the lens through which we understand the sociopolitical engagement of Native peoples with the administrative systems of the colonizer. It seems that we can draw a line from the knowledge produced by what Rifkin calls "treaty subjectivity" to the knowledge produced (or lack thereof) about the sociopolitical arrangements of the Sandusky people. Treaty subjectivity is the practice of "producing bureaucratically workable forms of subjectivity." Treaty subjectivities "define what constitutes native collective voice in ways that make federal governance possible, tactically reconciling or deferring jurisdictional struggles while legitimizing the imperial absorption of native lands as part of the normal, constitutional, and consensual operation of national law."[8]

The representational habits of federal political engagement with natives, especially with those natives seen as occupying "frontier" spaces, sought a native collective voice on settler terms. Those terms generated subjectivities in and around treaties, which sought to rearrange local ways of politically organizing community decisions. Scholars, too many to mention here, have noted the ways in which Euro-Americans misinterpreted the sociopolitical organization of native peoples. More interesting than simply a misstep of the colonizer, this miscommunication is a source for understanding the ways in which natives represented themselves in ongoing political negotiations with settler administrative tactics and refused a treaty subjectivity. It is in the local forms of representation where we see community logics extend to interaction with colonial administration. This extension of local principles is always and already a refusal of treaty subjectivity—a refusal of organizational subjectivities imposed by the treaty process. Through the lens of treaty subjectivity, the Sandusky people appear as highly disorganized due to their lack of "national" and consistent representation. Locally, however, the fluctuating leadership represented at treaty negotiations, for example, points to a decentralized, kinship-based form of representation more resembling the undifferentiated social institutions predating the nineteenth-century aggressive tactics of colonial administration.

Local forms of representation show the ways the community was collectively representing its values in colonial political engagement, which leads me to ask: what if the political engagement by the Sandusky people was simply the vehicle for representing their values in the processes of colonial administration? This very question disrupts conventional understanding of how Ohio Indian communities were to have been engaged in a process of negotiation where the representational habits of the federal government served as the institutional default. The individuals who engaged the federal political system as representational vehicles of community values were not empowered with the ability to speak for the community. Rather, they were extensions of the autonomous community relationships—between people, the longhouse, and other cosmic entities—as it was understood by the Sandusky people.[9] Engagement in the treaty process, from the Sandusky people's perspective, was clearly one where the logic of the Longhouse prevailed. Considering the proposals of the settler state, as with any decision-making process guided by the principles of the Longhouse, would take time and patience to negotiate intracommunity politics and desires. Making decisions would require multiple forms of internal and external engagement with values through social practices, such as ceremonies and councils.

COUNCIL SUBJECTIVITIES

The Sandusky people's handling of aggressive settlement lies in contrast to government attempts to formulate a bureaucratically effective subjectivity for them through treaty negotiations. From the perspective of Indian agents, territorial officials, and the U.S. executive branch, the Sandusky people were unpredictable, unreliable, and duplicitous in their dealings around removal. Thus, in order to succeed in securing land cessions and removal, the Indian bureaucracy had to create an institution providing subjective resolution to the problems in dealing with decentralized representational political systems. Prevailing sentiment among officials interpreted an apparent indecisiveness among community leaders as a stalling tactic meant to disrupt U.S. attempts at reaching an agreement for land cessions and removal. Fluctuating leadership, native-stated unsuitability of proposed land in Indian Territory, and unreasonable financial requests were all seen as ways the Sandusky people attempted to forestall removal by complicating treaty negotiations. At the same time, the Sandusky people consistently, over a fourteen-year period, attended meetings with government officials, from local agents to the president, to discuss possible solutions to the effects of settlement on their people and settlers' desire for native-held lands. Meetings with U.S. officials produced letters, translated orations, interstitial agreements, and the foundations of what would eventually become the 1831 removal treaty. The consistent engagement in the bureaucratic structure of removal tells us of an ongoing process where the Sandusky people sought to make the best arrangements possible for their community. Their continued political engagement also provides evidence of a collective commitment to values whereby the logic of the Longhouse is extended to the settler state through a "council subjectivity."

The word *council* appears frequently in bureaucratic documents referencing meetings between native community representatives and U.S. officials. *Council*, from the federal government's perspective, was a moniker for an event where discussions and negotiations took place and terms were developed into treaties. Historically, Iroquois councils contained these activities as well and were crucial to continued good relations with neighboring peoples. For federal bureaucrats, however, "the council" was simply a stand-in phrase for a particular kind of Euro-American diplomatic negotiation.

In contrast, the Iroquois embodied the councils they held with Euro-Americans with principles focused on process and autonomous decision-making, as they had for centuries. Councils were the primary political embodiment of Iroquois values and served to ensure respectful community engagement internally as well as to frame engagement with alien peoples. The socioreligious foundation for the nineteenth-century treaty councils came from the "Great Peace," when, in the late-sixteenth and early-seventeenth centuries, the ten or so Iroquois villages ceased the practice of attacking one another and taking population-replenishing captives in mourning wars. Out of the Great Peace came the Condolence Ceremony, a symbolic redirection of the blood revenge which produced a kinship-inspired system of political continuity and collective aegis.

The Condolence Ceremony is but one form of the council complex among the Iroquois, but the most important given its influence on all other council practices. The Condolence Council functioned primarily as a mourning ritual and provided for the succession of chiefs, and continues as such today.[10] As the first cross-community set of etiological beliefs and political functions, the Condolence Council established etiquette, principles, and fundamental dispositions for engagement in discussion, debate, and decision-making. Whether a council was held at the clan level or representatives of all the Iroquois villages were meeting at the Grand Council, the fundamental values of duality and reciprocity were used to ensure continued good relations and positive decision-making.

Duality framed Iroquois solutions to problems; for example, outsiders should be adopted so as to bring them into kin relations and resolve the inherent conflict between local and stranger. Reciprocity was necessary to resolve tensions between dualities, and thus to make an outsider kin required a generosity to the outsider and others among the locals who would be expected to accept the person. Duality was a state of mind where the "clear-minded" contrasted with the "down-minded," who were individuals suffering from grief. Reciprocity of material items and spiritual well-wishes in the form of good thoughts functioned to lift the down-minded and restore normal relations.

By resolving the dyads of community life, the model of the Condolence Ceremony infused other council proceedings with a focus on calming tensions, reaching consensus, and promoting "clear-mindedness."[11] The Sandusky people most likely viewed their ongoing engagement with the U.S. federal Indian bureaucracy through their long cultural history of councils and with the condolence ceremony as their primary supernatural guide. This orientation would require them to proceed in their negotiations with a collectively clear mind and reciprocity. As a basic structure for diplomatic relations for engaging outsiders, the condolence rituals would have governed the Sandusky people's interactions with federal representatives with the goal of maintaining peace. Peace, in this sense, is not merely the absence of violence or war, but an emotional state where deliberate, well-thought-out action prevailed over the course of multiple thoughtful interactions.[12] The federal treaty system, and the subjectivities it produced, were not designed to accommodate the patient and consensual approach of American Indian political diplomacy.[13]

A typical council would begin with the parties recognizing their duality by seating themselves on opposite sides of the fire. Before actual negotiations began, condolence rituals were performed to recognize the mourning of the visiting party and resolve any prior conflicts. Relevant local histories were presented as a means to contextualize the problem at hand and no doubt reaffirm each party's interest in maintaining peace. After condolences were offered and ritual introductions made, proposals were offered by the party calling for a council. Each proposal, accompanied by a gift, was carefully laid out. No formal answers were given after the initial presentation of the proposed action or agreements. Rather, answers came only after extensive deliberation among leaders and additional councils. Another council would be called at a later time for delivering answers or further negotiations. Given the gravity of the decision to cede lands and remove, it is likely that the Sandusky people held many councils and deliberated extensively about various aspects of treaty agreements. Their habit of bringing proposals to the community, deliberating, and returning to federal authorities for further negotiation and clarifications frustrated Indian agents who sought a quick resolution to "the Indian problem." The ongoing negotiations, however, illustrate a community commitment to a locally conceived process, one where Iroquois ideas about responsibility and clear-mindedness prevailed.

Council subjectivity shifts the analysis away from seeing the fourteen-year period between the 1817 treaty and removal as a series of moves to stall the inevitable toward a recognition of the ongoing negotiations as a thoughtful political process guided by the fundamental principles of Iroquois diplomatic engagement. Throughout this period the federal government attempted to enforce treaty subjectivity as a matter of policy. Yet the Sandusky people continued their community's diplomacy through practices insuring the sustainability of their autonomy and clear-mindedness. Ironically, a council subjectivity would, by design, respect the autonomy of the settler state. As a powerful political and social rival, the United States would have required respectful engagement so as to not upset the clear-mindedness of proceedings and to ensure continued peace. In order to successfully negotiate and proceed with a clear mind, the Sandusky people would be required to do their best at making family with the federal authorities, which was most often achieved through kin-termed language, such as *father, children,* and *brother.* Seeking clear-minded resolutions to settler and native desires did not set well with the federal system's need for a one-time meeting to agree to terms. Instead, negotiating Sandusky community values turned out to be a single fourteen-year council of deliberate and patient negotiation designed to ensure peace.

A FOURTEEN-YEAR COUNCIL

In March of 1817, a few months before the Treaty at Maumee Rapids, Acting Secretary of War George Graham sent a letter to Michigan Territory Governor Lewis Cass, notifying him of President Monroe's desire "to make an effort to extinguish the Indian title to all the lands now claimed by them within the limits of the State of Ohio."[14] Cass was instructed to seek out the chiefs and headmen of Ohio tribes to ascertain their openness to ceding all or a portion of their lands and under what terms cessions might be possible. The president and the War Department desired a strategically important clear path between Ft. Meigs and the more easterly areas of Ohio. Graham emphasized: "The removal of the Indians, generally, from the vicinity of Lake Erie, and the advantages that would be derived from connecting the population of the State of Ohio with that of the Michigan Territory, give to the acquisition of this country a political importance that would justify a more liberal compen-

sation for its relinquishment than has hitherto been given for the relinquishment of Indian claims."[15] Graham was conveying the president's "at
all costs" desire to have a native-free and loyal settler corridor between
the established East and the sociopolitically weaker Western territories.
Cass included the Sandusky people in a series of trips to visit various
communities of Ohio Indians, such as the Wyandotte and Miami, from
whom he was directed to procure the entirety of their "title." Unable
to persuade community leaders to dispense with all of their property,
Cass had to settle for negotiating the cession of key pieces of land in
the upper and middle Sandusky region. Despite frustrations with the
Ohio Indians' demands for goods and annuities, Cass's meetings bore
fruit as he was able to negotiate the cession of large tracts of land for
both settlement and military installations with all of the Ohio Indians
in a single treaty.[16]

The negotiations that produced the treaty and cessions of 1817
set in motion a new era of intense interaction between the U.S. federal
bureaucracies and the Ohio peoples. The Ohio communities' allegiance
to the British in the War of 1812 continued to prioritize the rapid settlement of the Ohio and Michigan lands. Settlers created a much-needed
buffer between foreign nations and lesser-known and little-trusted Indians. Through rumor and field reports it was clear to War Department
officials that the Ohio Indians maintained contact with British traders
and officials in Canada well into the 1820s.[17] In order to ensure the
newly acquired allegiance of the Indians to the United States, and their
removal, federal officials desired a centralized government representing
the various "tribes" with whom they were negotiating. The federal government's goal of rapidly moving natives west required a consistent and
helpful Indian leadership and thus blinded bureaucrats to the reality of
most communities' council-based political systems. For the federal government, every meeting with Indians that did not produce a removal
treaty was a failure on the part of Ohio peoples to be rational, fair, and
objective. However, in the post-1817 councils, we see each meeting
providing an opportunity for Sandusky leaders to obtain proposals from
U.S. officials and bring the information back to the people for deliberation in community and clan meetings where local understandings and
political process prevailed. Thus, when the Sandusky people met with
Cass for the first time in 1817 concerning the cession of their lands,
they most likely understood it as a continuation of an ongoing and
developing negotiation; one with no clearly definable beginning or end.
Cass was seen by President Monroe's staff as somewhat unsuccessful in

obtaining only a portion of the Ohio lands, and federal officials were continuously frustrated with expenditures in gifts, food, and travel support for meetings producing only expanded native demands and rejections of U.S. proposals. Ohio peoples expected gifts, deliberations, and a degree of ceremonialism when conducting a series of councils with anybody, including federal authorities. Negotiations more easily broke down when established protocols were not followed or when federal authorities appeared too eager for answers and agreements.

By extending council values to these negotiations, the Sandusky people actively engaged the process from a core set of cultural logics rather than reactively creating new or hybrid (middle-ground) cultural forms. In an effort to promote clear-mindedness, the Sandusky community, as an aspect of council subjectivity, extended kinship to federal authorities. The use of terms such as *Father* or *Great Father* to refer to the U.S. government or the president is often thought of as a form of U.S. government paternalism.[18] However, the council complex among the Iroquois, and the Condolence council in particular, made extensive use of kinship terms, relations, and the values of a kinship-based political system. No doubt Indian agents and other bureaucrats viewed native peoples through a patriarchal paternalism. Yet, in a council setting, a state of peace required Sandusky people to extend relations of kinship to the other party. Kinship and other values contained in the councils held by the Sandusky people with federal negotiators illustrate the practice of extended and thoughtful interaction required by the Iroquois decision-making process. The thoughtful interaction provided a basis for their firmness in making their desires known.

In 1818 agent Johnston was instructed to begin serious work on removing the Wyandotte, Seneca, and Shawnee west of the Mississippi. He wrote the following after delivering a proposal to those three communities:

> In the execution however of this branch of our instructions we considered it neither politick [sic] nor just in any manner to urge their acceptance of our proposition. We submitted it to them in a way not to awaken their jealousies, nor alarm their fears and yet so that we could expect their fair opinions respecting it. The result was a prompt and I may add an indignant rejection of the offer and we were ultimately convinced that the mode in which the proposition reached them was the most fortunate, which could have been selected. A direct request to them would

perhaps have caused their immediate departure from this place and I am perfectly confident that nothing but the application of physical force can for a few years compel them to leave the country which they have inherited from their fore fathers.[19]

As the immediate rejection of a removal proposal so soon after the 1817 treaty shows, a patient process is not a capitulative one. Rather, it is one where confidence is built through successive instances of clear-minded interaction, negotiation, and recognition of community autonomy. However, federal authorities' weariness with the Sandusky people's deliberate approach continually threatened peaceful interactions.

Every annuity distribution and visit by an Indian agent involved a discussion of removal, community grievances with settlers, and the administration of reservation economics. These meetings might take place at the community longhouse, a leader's house, or at the agency headquarters. Communities would send individuals to these council-like meetings to collect annuities and goods due under treaty obligation. In the process of transferring money, livestock, dry goods, and other stores, the Indian agent would attempt to ascertain the community's disposition toward land cessions and removal. Community representatives would seek to clear their minds by discussing settler depredations on their land and violations of the treaty agreements as well as more serious charges of assaults and murders by settlers and neighboring native communities.

Agents most often returned from these meetings with little progress toward removal and harsh words from agency Indians frustrated with the government's refusal to meet treaty obligations and protect the community from settlers. Dissatisfaction grew as reports of native reluctance to remove found their way up the chain of command to the president. The government's failure to remedy the Sandusky people's grievances no doubt made them reluctant to engage in serious negotiation for removal. From their perspective, the government—the people with whom they had made every attempt to hold clear-minded councils—had done little to ensure 'peace' by failing to alleviate the anxieties of living under colonial administration. Meeting the financial, political, and economic obligations of treaties would have been a sign of federal clear-mindedness and meaningful negotiation. Being met with only demands and no recompense at a council would have told the Seneca leaders that federal authorities were not negotiating in earnest and would not have inspired the Sandusky people to take any significant action or seriously consider government proposals. Instead, the Sandusky people would refuse to consider government proposals until they were certain of a peaceful solution.

Indian agents and other officials recognized why Ohio Indians would be reluctant to leave their "homelands," but at the same time were confused by stiff-necked opposition to removal amid the onslaught of settlers. In 1822 agent Johnston noted that the "Seneca are or soon will be surrounded with settlements of our citizens."[20] The Sandusky people no doubt also recognized the incompatibility between their desire to continue to live by the principles they cherished and the demands on them from the settler state. Whether it was the 1820 proposal of a state road through the reservation or the persistent encroachment of settlers on their land and hunting rights, the Sandusky people were in a continual state of negotiation for the autonomy of their physical and cultural space.[21] A clear pattern of settler exploitation emerged, such as the theft of livestock and other items by settlers who trespassed onto the reservation. Despite turning a blind eye to settler encroachments, agents and War Department bureaucrats continued to make demands for removal negotiations.[22]

The patient approach of the Sandusky, as well as other Ohio peoples, was not inactive by any means. Rather, Iroquois communities in New York, Ohio peoples, and peoples already self-removed to Indian Territory, primarily Delaware and Cherokee Old Settlers, had been communicating with one another and exchanging wampum about possibilities for sharing reservations in the West. The translocated peoples already occupying Indian Territory were motivated by the need for increased numbers to defend themselves against hostilities from the Osage and other natives indigenous to the area who controlled the best hunting grounds and the most valuable resources. The New York and Michigan Superintendency Indians were motivated by the continued encroachment of settlers and federal government neglect. A coalition among these three groups would no doubt strengthen their ability to negotiate.[23] By the mid-1820s representatives of the Six Nations in New York State were engaging Indian agents in both the Northeast and the Michigan Superintendency, hoping to locate "a new home." Their intent was to relocate in Ohio with the Seneca of Sandusky or the Seneca-Shawnee in Lewistown and join them for their removal west. The Oneida, in particular, were seeking to move to Ohio, but federal authorities were reluctant to allow more communities to occupy Ohio lands given the government's intent of removing all natives in the south Great Lakes region.[24]

By 1823 the loose coalition of Western, Ohio, and Six Nations peoples was ready to engage federal authorities in a formal council negotiation. A series of preliminary councils were held to obtain the Ohio Indians' participation in a "Great Council." The Sandusky Seneca were to host the council. As Superintendent of Indian Affairs William Clark states, "The principle object of the Council is to form an Alliance, and to propose a General Peace among all the Indians, and to inforce [sic] it on those nations who may be disposed not to listen to Reason and justice, to perfect the Removal and Settlement of all the Indians East of the Mississippi and South of Lake to the West Side."[25] The federal government was hopeful the Great Council would result in an agreement for the removal of all Ohio, New York, and Michigan Territory Indians west. Of particular interest to the communities that agreed to participate was to remove in a way in which "they may exact and enforce their own law and regulations necessary."[26] The proposed coalition, however, contained two differing perspectives on removal and its value to each community. The correspondence leading up to the council reveals a degree of reticence on the part of more culturally conservative Sandusky people versus a group of Ohio Indians who allied themselves with the Shawnee Chief Quatawapea, or with Colonel Lewis and the Shawnee Prophet, Tenskwatawa. Confusing the situation for both the Ohio natives and the federal government was the influence of Col. Lewis in organizing and guiding the proceedings of the council. Col. Lewis had served with the Americans during the War of 1812 and was a highly successful planter and businessman on the Seneca-Shawnee Reservation in Lewistown, Ohio. Col. Lewis was seen by some of his own people as a comprador to the settler state's politics and was recognized as an economic ally by Indian agents due to his interest in developing mining operations, promoting Jesuit education among his people, and the protection he provided for federal interests in the region.[27] William Clark acknowledged the necessity of a council to ensure a properly executed and representative decision. Col. Lewis's political savvy and Tenskwatawa's spiritual influence were his best options for realizing a productive meeting. He also clearly understood the difficulty of achieving a single mass migration from Western New York, Ohio, Tennessee, and Indiana. The council at Sandusky, as much as it was a necessity for conducting business among various communities, was also an attempt by William Clark to use the council cultural apparatus to orchestrate an audience for leaders favorable to removal and to influence the resisters. So certain was Clark of a positive result, on the word of Col. Lewis, that he had arranged for a deputation from the Six Nations to bring wampum to the Sandusky Council as well as prearranged travel for the entire deputation of Six Nations, Shawnee, Delaware, Seneca, Wyandotte, Miami, Ottawa, and Pottawatomie representatives to Washington, DC, a month later.[28] However, the council was very slow in coming. Two years after Clark's initial attempt to bring together a council, Lewis Cass, Superintendent Clark, and a delegation of Western Cherokee, Western Shawnee, and Ohio Shawnee met with community leaders at Wapakoneta, not Sandusky, in February 1825. The Shawnee leader Black Hoof, who opposed removal, also attended the meeting.

With the approval of Clark, Col. Lewis and the Cherokee delegation traveled from the Wapakoneta council to Washington to present their plan to President Monroe, who sent them back to St. Louis with his approval to proceed with a removal treaty for the Shawnee and other communities willing to join them. John Johnston returned from the meeting with President Monroe in Washington in April with doubts about the possibility of getting Sandusky and other Ohio communities' consent for a council and agreement. Federal officials' frustrations with the approach of the Sandusky and other Ohio headmen began to peak.[29] Piqua agent John Johnston put much of the blame on Clark and Cass's confidence in Col. Lewis. Johnston assessed the following in April of 1825: "I believe however there need be no beneficial result expected. The Indian Lewis who has continued this visit and the plan of removal is very unpopular with our Indians." In his letter to L. McKenney, Johnston goes on to tell how Lewis had used his position of chief to embezzle annuities to pay for improvements to his own land and business. As a result, the Shawnees "deposed" Col. Lewis and about one thousand moved to Indian Territory around the White River in Arkansas. Johnston tells McKenney that Lewis "is not confided in this country, nor will the Indians in Ohio listen to him."

William Clark, however, had a great deal of faith in Col. Lewis and his ability to deliver a signed treaty of removal from the Great Council at Wapakoneta. Johnston, however, having extensive experience with the Sandusky peoples and the sociopolitical practices of the council, knew the council planned for Wapakoneta would fail. More importantly, Johnston recognized that "There was not a person in the deputation who had the shadow of authority to act for the Indians of Ohio."[30] None of the individuals selected by government officials and Col. Lewis to go to Washington had actually obtained the approval to negotiate any form of removal agreement, much less hold preliminary councils with the government. Johnston knew that the Sandusky peoples "will act for themselves and when the proper time comes will request permission to send a deputation to Washington to make the necessary arrangements."[31] Johnston correctly predicted the outcome of the May 1825 council at Wapakoneta. When Col. Lewis and the Cherokee delegation returned, Black Hoof had developed an anti-removal coalition among the Shawnee and other Ohio peoples. By the time Col. Lewis had returned, the Shawnee Prophet had changed his position and allied with Black Hoof.

The 1825 Council was universally recognized as a failure by Clark, the President, and others in favor of Indian removal. However, the Wapokoneta council and the Washington council left no doubt of the government's impatience for the removal of the Sandusky people. Prompted by the councils, a group of Sandusky leaders traveled to Indian Territory to explore possible relocation sites. Three headmen, Seneca Steel, Comstock, and Cracked Hoof, set out on horseback to Indian Territory to investigate the suitability of lands in and around the area already occupied by the Cherokee Old Settlers and the Osage. The men were gone for nearly a year and held councils with numerous communities already occupying what would be Northeast Oklahoma.[32] While they were gone, Indian agents continued to attempt to negotiate removal with the headmen who remained on the reservation. The years between their departure in 1825 and their return to negotiations in 1828 mark a critical political moment at Sandusky, where leaders found themselves at a critical tipping point brought on by the desire for community autonomy, state pressure for removal, and the desires of their very own kin.

AUTONOMY, REPRESENTATION AND THE MURDER OF SENECA JOHN

Seneca John, the brother of headman Coonstick, was himself caught in a particular convergence of community attempts to remain autonomous, structures of authority, and the increasing influence of removal pressures. The result for Seneca John was tragic. On a winter morning in 1828 a group of Seneca of Sandusky headmen met him outside his brother's house, drove a hatchet into his head, and cut his throat, an act to which he freely submitted.[33] The following is an excerpt of events as told to settler Henry Howe by Indian subagent Henry Brish:

> About the year 1825, Coonstick, Steel and Cracked Hoof left
> the reservation for the double purpose of a three years hunting

and trapping excursion, and to seek a location for a new home for the tribe in the far West.

At the time of their starting, Comstock, the brother of the first two, was the principal chief of the tribe. On their return in 1828, richly laden with furs and horses, they found Seneca John, their fourth brother, chief, in place of Comstock, who had died during their absence.

Comstock was the favorite brother of the two, and they at once charged Seneca John with producing his death by witchcraft. John denied the charge in a strain of eloquence rarely equalled. Said he, "I loved my brother Comstock more than I love the green earth I stand upon. I would give myself, limb by limb, piecemeal by piecemeal—I would shed my blood, drop by drop to restore him to life." But all his protestations of innocence and affection for his brother Comstock were of no avail. His two other brothers pronounced him guilty and declared their determination to be his executioners.

John replied that he was willing to die and only wished to live until the next morning, "to see the sun rise once more." This request being granted, John told them that he should sleep that night on Hard Hickory's porch, which fronted the east, where they would find him at sunrise. He chose that place because he did not wish to be killed in the presence of his wife, and desired that the chief, Hard Hickory, should witness that he died like a brave man.

Coonstick and Steel retired for the night to an old cabin nearby. In the morning, in company with Shane, another Indian, they proceeded to the house of Hard Hickory, who was my informant of what there happened.

He said, a little after sunrise he heard their footsteps upon the porch, and opened the door just enough to peep out. He saw John *asleep* upon his blanket, while they stood around him. At length one of them awoke him. He arose upon his feet and took off a large handkerchief which was around his head, letting his unusually long hair fall upon his shoulders. This being done, he looked around upon the landscape and at the rising sun, to take a farewell look of a scene that he was never again to behold and then told them he was ready to die.

Shane and Coonstick each took him by the arm, and Steel walked behind. In this way they led him about ten steps from the porch, when Steel struck him with a tomahawk on the back of his head, and he fell to the ground, bleeding freely. Supposing this blow sufficient to kill him, they dragged him under a peach tree near by. In a short time, however, he revived; the blow having been broken by his great mass of hair. Knowing that it was Steel who struck the blow, John, as he lay, turned his head towards Coonstick and said, "Now brother, do you take your revenge." This so operated upon the feelings of Coonstick, that he interposed to save him; but it enraged Steel to such a degree, that he drew his knife and cut John's throat from ear to ear, and the next day he was buried with the usual Indian ceremonies, not more than twenty feet from where he fell. Steel was arrested and tried for the murder in Sandusky County, and acquitted.

The grave of Seneca John was surrounded by a small picket enclosure. Three years after, when I was preparing to move them to the far West, I saw Coonstick and Steel remove the picket-fence and level the ground, so that no vestige of the grave remained.[34]

The case against the men who killed Seneca John appeared before the Ohio Territory Supreme Court in 1829, two years before their removal to Indian Territory. The reason the killers gave in their defense was that Seneca John had violated community rules by presenting himself as chief in the absence of the local leaders. The headmen also told the judge that Seneca John had murdered Comstock through witchcraft so as to become chief. The Ohio judge found that the "Seneca Council" was acting within their jurisdiction and rules of their community. The recognition by the judge of the Seneca headmen's authority evokes a pre-Marshall-decision acknowledgement of sovereignty.

More important to the discussion here, however, is the acceptance of witchcraft accusations as a plausible reason for murder. The murdering of witches was not unheard of among the Ohio communities and had occurred several times on the Sandusky reservation. It is unremarkable that the Sandusky people, as culturally conservative believers in the execution of witches, would murder one of their own for witchcraft. In 1822, during an epidemic of illness causing multiple deaths on the reservation, four women were "tomahawked" for witchcraft. The community held a council and determined the four witches had spread sickness to the people. The day after the council, the four women drank whisky until they were drunk and then submitted to the execution. Iroquois traditions warn about the disruptive and dangerous power of various kinds of witches and their effect on clear-mindedness and the social order. We do not know for certain if the requirement of witch execution in the Code of Handsome Lake had influenced Sandusky Iroquois thinking or whether they were adhering to more ancient notions about the treatment of social disrupters.[35] Nevertheless, witches were put to death throughout the reservation period and beyond removal.

The execution of witches at Sandusky appears to be exclusively among women until the death of Seneca John. Matthew Dennis in *Seneca Possessed* tells us that the violence surrounding the witch hunts "was less a matter of traditional practice than it was a function of the Seneca's tacit acceptance of Euro-American misogyny. Seeing witchcraft as a female art was ironically a measure of 'progress.'"[36] Dennis makes an overwhelmingly convincing argument about the ways in which patriarchy seeped into Iroquois sociopolitical life and the ways witches came to embody the search for power. Additionally, witches and witchcraft allegations, in a different community setting and different temporal scape, reveal the ways witchcraft accusations may have also been a response to the pressures of settlement. No doubt the judge in the Seneca John murder saw a "measure of progress" in the execution of a community member for witchcraft; he was recognizing "modernity among the savages." Within the community, however, witchcraft was an explanation for disruptions in the social order. That is, the witchcraft allegations against Seneca John were a potential form of resistance to his standing in the way of the "one mind" among the Sandusky peoples. The "protocol of public councils suppresses latent hostility, and the devices employed for attaining unanimity overcome factionalism," which Seneca John's actions undermined. Seneca John's witchcraft may have not been supernatural, but instead disrupted the natural order of the Sandusky people's decision-making processes. The murder of Seneca John was no doubt precipitated indirectly by pressures to cede land for settlement and previous government attempts to subvert council-based sociopolitical decision-making. Seneca John himself knew he had undermined the council system when he stepped into the grass for execution. Witchcraft, quite possibly, in Seneca John's case, was the act of breaking moral community by acting in ways that undermined the authority, autonomy, and subjectivity of the council. The leaders who were away in Indian Territory appeared to be, from all descriptions, attempting to accumulate information and evidence (returning with pelts, hides, and trade goods) in order to make a clear-minded decision with the community. Seneca John, however, seems to have begun acting on his own by representing the community as an individual and not as a human extension of the Longhouse. From our theoretical vantage point, we can see Seneca John's murder as a way of speaking to the colonizer—of making colonial administrators aware of their failure to penetrate community social relations. The execution also serves to reinforce the importance of a council subjectivity and certain community leaders' mortal commitment to its principles.

FOUR

DISPLACING THE LONGHOUSE

To remove the Senecas of Sandusky, Ohio . . . afforded me an opportunity of aiding in the benevolent policy of removing the Indians to a
country better adapted to their habits and necessities, and of providing for those immediately under my charge such comforts upon their
journey as they had been accustomed to.

—Henry Brish to William Clark, August 31, 1833

The return of the headmen from Indian Territory and the death of Seneca John marked a turning point in the Sandusky people's engagement
with removal. It is unclear what precipitated the increased interaction
of headmen with Indian agents, but by late 1828 Sandusky headmen
were actively seeking councils with the president and other authorities
to discuss the possibilities of removal. In a letter to Andrew Jackson
from an administrative embassy of nineteen Sandusky men, Martin Lane
interpreted the following in 1830:

> Our Great Father is again requested to give his red children his
> ear. They sent him a year ago their application informing him
> of their desire to dispose of their reservation on the Sandusky
> River in Ohio and their wish to go away beyond the Mississippi.
> They have received no answer to their request—They are fear-
> ful that their Great Father has not been made acquainted with
> their wishes. His red children are now more anxious than ever to
> emigrate—They wish to exchange their Lands here for others on
> the west side of the Mississippi—The game is destroyed around
> their Lands in Ohio and their young people are daily learning
> bad habits from the white people—They therefore wish to leave

this country as soon as their Great Father will allow them to exchange their Lands and give them the means of departing for their new home.[1]

The federal government's inability to successfully manage, fund, and support the reservation system is widely known. Indian Affairs, in all of its bureaucratic manifestations, never fully provided for reservation Indians according to treaty agreements, which only made communities more vulnerable to the constant assault from settlers who viewed natives as conquered peoples whose resistance to American national advancement impeded their God-given rights.[2] From the 1817 treaty through the time of removal, annuities guaranteed by treaty to the Sandusky people went mostly unpaid or only partially paid. Basic rations of various sorts, such as beef, pork, flour, and sugar, arrived in minuscule quantities or in unusable condition from rot to ruin. Pleading letters from Johnston to multiple superiors detail the crises caused by delayed or nonexistent annuities and subsistence items guaranteed under previous treaties.[3]

Obviously, the violation of treaty agreements, settler pressures, and cultural preservation were important factors for the Sandusky people's decision to remove. What we must understand, however, is that the Sandusky people, not the federal government, decided when to sign the removal treaty. The Sandusky people themselves, no doubt with the eager encouragement of Piqua agent Johnston and Superintendent Clark, contacted the president and agreed to travel to Washington, D.C., to execute the agreement.

The details of the removal treaty were fifteen years in the making. The multiple councils and negotiations that had taken place between 1817 and 1831 provided the foundation for the removal agreement, but also tell of a complex process whereby the Sandusky people continually sought to maintain their autonomy. As a process whereby the Indian bureaucracy engaged autonomous sociocultural communities, removal— the events leading up to relocation, the treaty negotiations, and the move itself—generated a community situatedness. Community situatedness was informed by community culture but was also determined in the field of engagement where the settled and the settler met. Removal has thus far been analyzed in three ways: as an extension of the settler state's powers, settler procedure, and the tragic outcomes of removal. All three are aspects of removal and are crucial in understanding its complexities. As a dialogical context, however, removal is situated by the multiple forms of knowledge brought to bear on settlers' displacement of indigenous peoples and thus a reality situated socially, politically, and temporally.[4]

Removal is a particular positionality where multiple axes of power converge to make it necessary and possible. Donna Haraway tells us that the "search for . . . a 'full' and total position is the search for the fetishized perfect subject of oppositional history . . ." and "subjugation is not grounds for etiology."[5] Thus, analyzing removed peoples, and the Sandusky people, as occupying a position of "victim" ignores the possibility of an autonomous etiological orientation for settled indigenous peoples. In order to avoid fetishizing the subjectivities produced by removal into a totalized victim, we must recognize the subjugated individual, and community, as not wholly settled by the colonizer. One is not wholly part of a subjugated group at all times. Instead, I propose that removal is a process emanating from a confluence of community contexts—community as well as settler knowledges informed by community and settler desires. The pressures applied by colonial administrators are implicated in the process, but so too are the ways in which natives filtered the process through local cultural logics. Removal as a subject position reveals the temporary moment of translocation—the year of travel between Sandusky and Neosho—at the same time it allows for the possibility of continuity. Removal as a moment of sociopolitical domination also provided a moment in which the Sandusky people could make their own subject-position as self-directed action and simultaneously a refusal to attach themselves to the structure seeking to limit their autonomy.[6] Removal produces two potential forms of subjectivity—the subject *in* removal and the subject *of* removal. The removed subject *in* removal is not unified "but a construction and a process, a heterogeneity, and intersection."[7] The subject *of* removal experiences multiple forms of subjective unity: first, of its own sociopolitical-cultural arrangements, and second, the unity of the indigenous subject as it exists in the ethics and policies of the settler. The subject *of* removal is of the second kind, a position generated by knowledge about indigenous peoples by the settler state—for example, the notion of the savage bound by tradition and resistant to progress. In contemporary terms, the subject *of* removal is a tragic figure overrun and detrimentally transformed by the power and will of the settler state.

In this chapter I seek to present the possibility of the Sandusky people as the subject *in* removal which is of its own sociopolitical arrangements. It is probable that removal challenged the sociocultural unity of the Sandusky people's society, but the transformation was guided as much by community subjectivity as by the subjectivities of the colonizer. Community subjectivity stands in contrast and sociopolitical opposition to the settler state's attempt to formulate a transformed subjectivity for natives by relocating them. Transformation as the result of translocation is not wholesale, and transformations do not negate the continuation and unity of cultural logics or the practices that emanate from them. Removal, in this way, is a process among many processes encountered by a colonized society that uses its community values as a means of sociopolitical engagement. Thus, removal among the Sandusky peoples was thought-out, negotiated, contested, and realized through the logic of their Longhouse.

It was clearly a contentious process, and by no means is my analysis attempting to romanticize away community conflict, greed, and individualistic behavior. Nor am I attempting to disengage the intensely violent and destructive forces of settlement, removal, and colonial policy. The real human suffering of removal and the state's violence against indigenous peoples occurred in multiple confluences of sociopolitical arrangements. In what I outline below, removal as a moment is a subject-position in space and time, created by a set of corporeal and social experiences understood through elements of an ancient cultural apparatus. As we saw autonomy and clear-mindedness as the guiding principles for community engagement, we also see these values in removal as a multifaceted experience rather than a submission to the policies of the settler state. Thinking through these principles allows us to conceive of the Sandusky peoples' removal as a moment of community engagement and another moment in cultural continuity.

The Emigrating Seneca

In October of 1829 the Piqua agent John McElvain and the "Seneca Chiefs" sponsored a three-day council at Sandusky where leaders of surrounding communities gathered to discuss and renew financial agreements from previous treaties. The Sandusky leaders also used the council to "prevail upon them [leaders from surrounding communities] to dispose of their possessions and all to emigrate together to the West next season."[8] Most of the agents present at the council interpreted the Sandusky people's desire to remove as an indication of their willingness to become civilized. However, agent McElvain, who had many years of experience with natives in Ohio, recognized removal as an "arrangement to prevent their entire annihilation, which appears to me certain under the present system of hemming them in narrow bound on small reservations."[9]

At the council, the Sandusky leaders failed to persuade other Piqua Agency communities, such as the Wyandotte and Shawnee, to join them in removal. The council did, however, provide the opportunity for Sandusky leaders to plead their case before President Jackson in a letter translated and penned by interpreter Martin Lane. The 1829 letter, despite being filtered through the interpreter and the desires of Indian agents to secure removal, speaks from a position of engagement by emphasizing removal as a means of community preservation. Nowhere in this letter or in any others from Sandusky leaders is there an expressed desire to alter their society by becoming frontier agriculturalists. Instead, the stated purpose of removal, in keeping with the teachings of Handsome Lake, is to "be out of the way of bad white men, and from strong drink, which has destroyed many of our people."[10] The availability of game-rich land, distance from settlers, and close proximity to other natives, such as the Cherokee, were consistent concerns of Sandusky leaders and justification for trading the Ohio reservation for lands in Indian Territory. Even removal as the preservation of culture is embedded in the imaginative manipulation of a state-sponsored agenda; we see through the actions of community members an interest in finding a solution to the pressure of settlement. From the perspective of the previous chapter emphasizing council subjectivity and an ongoing sociopolitical relationship with the settler state, we can think of the Sandusky leaders' letter-writing campaign and sudden eagerness to remove as the result of many years of clear-minded and deliberate negotiations. Through multiple councils, deliberations, and ceremony, the Sandusky leaders sought to think about removal through the logic of their Longhouse.

Among the signers of letters to the president are recognized community leaders, such as Tall Chief, Blue Jacket, Seneca Steel, Hard Hickory, and Coonstick. Most letters have either six or twelve signers, possibly indicating one or two persons from each of the six Seneca clans. Any recognition of clans through government documents is purely speculation, but the evidence clearly supports community endorsement of the leaders sponsoring the pre-removal councils and the probability of removal being a community-led strategy. The Sandusky headmen again held a council with Piqua Agency bureaucrats in 1830 and again dictated a letter to President Jackson, requesting his attention to their sad state and desire for removal. As before, many of the same headmen cited the need for the community to preserve itself from the pressures of settlement and their desire to live outside of the influence of white encroachment.[11]

Letters from Sandusky headmen to President Adams in 1828 and to President Jackson in 1829 and 1830, however, went unanswered, to the frustration of Superintendent Clark and the Piqua agents as well as the Sandusky leaders themselves. As described by agents McKenney, McElvain, and Johnston, the Sandusky leaders were becoming "anxious" and were accusing the agents of not transmitting their wishes to the president.[12]

Unbeknownst to the Sandusky leaders and oddly enough to the Indian agents themselves, their request was in perpetual suspension within the debate in Congress over Indian removal and the appropriations required to fund moving thousands of natives across the United States. Just one month before Congress passed the Indian Removal Act, Samuel Hamilton wrote to the Sandusky chiefs through John McElvain reassuring them of the president's desire to see them "gratified in their wishes" but informing them "the means have been asked for, but have not yet been granted by Congress."[13]

By the end of January 1831 the Sandusky peoples had yet to receive any further correspondence from the president's office or Superintendent Clark. Some eighty settler citizens of Seneca and Sandusky Counties in Ohio wrote to Congress in January of 1831 pleading for the fulfillment of the Sandusky Senecas' desire to remove. The settler's petition was of course in their best interest and drew on the standard language of a pro-removal political agenda by characterizing the Sandusky peoples as hard-drinking savages standing in the way of Manifest Destiny. The settlers were well informed of the goings-on at the reservation and were prompted to write the petition by news that some chiefs had taken upon themselves to travel to Washington, D.C., at their own expense.[14] On February 10, 1831, Comstick, Small Cloud Spicer, Seneca Steel, Hard Hickory, and Captain Good Hunter departed for Washington in the hope of meeting with the president. Agent McElvain sent a letter ahead to Colonel S. S. Hamilton in the hopes of making the president and his aides aware of the impending arrival of the chiefs. McElvain claimed to have discouraged the trip as he assured the chiefs they would not receive reimbursement for their travel or accommodations while in Washington. Brish, he speculated, had encouraged the chiefs to take matters into their own hands. McElvain was fearful the trip was "calculated to embarrass" the department.[15] Brish, it seems, was acting with one of the primary instigators of Indian removal from Ohio, James B. Gardiner, a retired colonel, publisher, and editor of various Ohio newspapers, and disgraced politician.[16] Gardiner was one of the many newspaper editors who supported the policies of President Jackson, particularly removal, and was appointed to various government positions by Jackson early in his administration.[17] Gardiner met with Andrew Jackson within the first few months of his presidency regarding settlement in Ohio. It is not surprising that Gardiner and Brish emerged as the political and financial facilitators of the Sandusky Chiefs' trip and the crafters of the agreement between the leaders and the federal government. Gardiner's help in securing the agreement earned him the appointment as Special Commissioner for Indian Affairs from President Jackson. Later in 1831 he would be given the responsibility of holding councils for removal treaties with all the Ohio Indians and the ability to negotiate terms on behalf of the president.[18]

Figure 4.1. *Good Hunter, a Warrior*. Date: 1872. Artist: George Catlin. Collection of the Smithsonian American Art Museum. Oil on canvas. Size: 21⅛ x 16½ in.

Figure 4.2. *Hard Hickory, an Amiable Man.* Date: 1872. Artist: George Catlin. Collection of the Smithsonian American Art Museum. Oil on canvas. Size: $21^{1}/_{8}$ x $16^{1}/_{2}$ in.

Nearly three weeks after arriving in Washington, the chiefs were successful in securing a removal treaty, which they signed on February 28, 1831. The treaty first stipulated a sale of their 40,000-acre reservation in Ohio and directed the proceeds from the sale to pay for a 67,000-acre reservation adjoining Western Cherokee lands and bordering the state of Missouri. Funds remaining after the government subtracted the costs of moving people and property, surveying the new land, and paying the contracts for the building of a blacksmith's shop, a gristmill, and a saw-mill would go into a fund from which future annuities would be paid.[19]

The leaders who had gone to Washington were so pleased with the result that after their return to Sandusky in April they sponsored a council to announce the provisions of the treaty and to begin discussions on preparing the community for removal. They invited all of the other communities under the Piqua Agency as well as the Seneca and Cayuga from the Six Nations in New York. Besides holding council meetings they also sponsored a thanksgiving ceremony at the longhouse to show their gratitude toward the "Great Spirit" for success in obtaining a treaty under such "agreeable conditions."[20] Later in the summer, around July, the signers of the treaty and other headmen from Sandusky attended what was most likely a Condolence Council with the Seneca in New York to return wampum before their departure to Indian Territory.[21]

The summer of 1831 was one occupied by numerous councils among the people overseen by the Piqua Agency. The list of expenditures for the councils reveals the significant resources devoted to enticing the other Ohio Indians to the negotiating table as well as managing the extensive logistical issues in moving an entire community cross-country. In May alone the Sandusky people, the Wyandotte, and the Delaware consumed fifteen pounds of tobacco for use in councils in addition to 1,000 pounds of bacon and seventy loaves of bread for one three-day council alone. The expenditures detail significant amounts of tobacco, meat, flour, and corn meal, and gifts of rifles, blankets, and livestock.[22]

May through July of 1831 saw at least seven councils held among multiple communities such as the Ottawa, Wyandotte, Sandusky, and Shawnee at the longhouses in Wapakoneta, Sandusky, and Lewistown. The various councils, seen as delays, were frustrating to Gardiner, who was attempting to balance the financial ineptness of the War Department, appropriation debates in Congress, and the communities' painfully slow approach to removal. Subagent Brish, it appears, was taking advantage of the convergence of the Sandusky people's eagerness to move, the influx of resources to the Piqua Agency funding removal, and the uncertainty around an actual departure date. McElvain consistently complained about Brish's habit of indulging the Sandusky people's wants, allowing delays caused by the community, and of fomenting discontent over the removal agreement.

To the dismay of Piqua agents, the Sandusky people, in expectation of an early removal, had not planted any crops in the spring. By mid-summer they were out of food and completely dependent upon the government for subsistence.[23] Initially, Brish seemed to be engaged in some form of sympathetic advocacy of the community, but a close examination reveals the subagent's diversion of commodities and exploitation of the Sandusky people's access to removal resources which, seemingly unknown to the community, were being extracted from their annuities. Brish had declared himself the sole representative of the Sandusky people, and according to McElvain, directed them in their requests for additional funds and supplies. Financial documents cited by McElvain show Brish's requests for additional wagons, firearms, blankets, and supplies, all of which were intended to support the Sandusky community. Yet, the rifles, blankets, and food were never delivered and were in fact repurchased twice during removal, once in St. Louis and again upon arrival in Indian Territory.[24]

Brish used delays to make further demands for resources by speaking on behalf of the community. In October of 1831 community members who were ready to move began encamping near Lewistown. Brish told the leaders they would require ten more horses and an additional ten wagons and directed the chiefs to request them from McElvain. It was later discovered that Brish had leased the horses and wagons for his own profit.

This is but one example of the ways Brish was following a post-treaty pattern among the various government-supported settler-agents and merchants surrounding reservations. Once word circulated on the amount of money paid to Ohio Indians for their lands and removal costs, merchants began making claims against the annuities. In the case of the Shawnee, one merchant was able to obtain the signature of several Shawnee headmen on a draft for $25,000 to settle the accounts of the tribe. McElvain, however, discovered the merchant only had documentation for $1,500 worth of supplies.[25]

McElvain and Gardiner were also prone to circular explanations for their own expenditure of resources and conflating costs associated with caring for the Piqua Agency's peoples. By the end of summer 1831, all of the agents were engaged in a power struggle over gaining the favor of the president in an attempt to obtain permanent government positions and the use of resources. Inevitably, the Sandusky people, particularly once they began traveling by land, bore the brunt of the pattern of exploitation and the agents' self-interested "good deeds."[26]

The process of removal, seemingly ready-made for the greed of settlers, was also complicated by the ways the Sandusky people functioned as a society. Despite the bureaucratic delays, agents' greedy exploitation of headmen, and the self-interested motives of settlers, the community found itself in a series of difficulties brought on by its cultural difference with the settler state. McElvain places blame on what he saw as negative characteristics of the Indian, but the difficulties experienced by the settler state reveal the ways the community continued to seek consensus and clear-mindedness in its decision to remove. McElvain complains to the president's secretary:

> The removal of the Senecas, owing to many causes, was more troublesome and expensive than was expected; as they have for some time been restless and unsettled in their minds.
>
> And notwithstanding they had expressed a wish to emigrate, still, when the time arrived that they must leave their ancient home, they shrunk back and were for some time at a stand, whether to seek a home in some other quarter or to emigrate to the land set apart for their future residence.
>
> When rightly understood, there was nothing unnatural in the intended separation of this band, as much contention prevails amongst its members principally owing to its being composed of several remnants or parts of nations, six or more in number. It is, therefore, easily seen that no common interest could long exist between such discordant materials, and I will venture to say, that there is not such another contrary and difficult people on the face of the earth (who pretend to live in one community) to do business with as this mixed band called Senecas. They have about thirty chiefs, each party a certain number, and each striving for the ascendency; and if failure takes place with either in council to carry a particular or favorite measure, murder is sure to follow.[27]

Community decisions were of course not without conflict. Certainly a number of Sandusky people were reluctant to move and accept the terms of the treaty. The summer councils and the significant delays tell us about a community that was still debating the benefits and costs of removal. They quite possibly were seeking alternatives to moving to Indian Territory by settling among another community closer to Ohio, as was believed by some of the Piqua agents. The Wyandotte, who were aggressively resisting removal, were encouraging the Sandusky peoples to reconsider the terms of their treaty and reside with them. As was observed by agents, the Wyandotte and the Sandusky peoples were heavily intermarried and at least a few Wyandotte leaders had "Seneca" wives.[28] Additionally, the extensive and contentious discussions among the chiefs of the "six nations" referenced above by McElvain were most likely held by the headmen chosen to convene council on behalf of clans and concerned when and if they should depart. For the community to relocate would require significant coordination as well as the proper set of ritual, political, and social considerations. In keeping with proper Longhouse traditions, and even more frustrating to McElvain and Gardiner, the community decided not to move until they had completed the Green Corn ceremony in August of 1831.[29]

The government's original plan was to remove all of the Sandusky people by steamboat.[30] However, about half of the population rejected the idea of traveling by water and instead chose to remove by land. Multiple agents noted the Piqua peoples' concerns about traveling by steamboat, chief among them a fear of explosions and raids by other tribes. However, as clearly stated by agents, individuals moving by steamship would not be able to move many of their household goods, which were to be sold to settlers and the proceeds transmitted to their owners at a later date. More than a fear of steamship travel, the desire to move on land was a practical solution to avoid extensive losses of property. Another interpretation of the community debate over steamboat versus land removal points to the possibility that the Sandusky people were divided about removal and those who were less enthusiastic used the land route as a way to locate a new home among other peoples along the way.

In September a group of about 200 people along with agent John McElvain departed and became known as the "land party." The land party proceeded slowly and lingered in Ohio and Indiana for a few months, visiting other communities along the route and holding councils and celebrations. McElvain complained to S. S. Hamilton about the expenditures for their frequent stops as the land group was holding council with multiple communities along the way and requested supplies to feed their hosts.[31] McElvain accompanied the land party until early November only as far as the Ohio border as he was certain they would make it to St. Louis by the end of winter. He left Martin Lane to see them through their journey. He further decided not to purchase any additional supplies, such as blankets or rifles, as he assumed their treaty provided for substantial provisions. It would take the land group two months for their wagon train to arrive in central Indiana, just south of "Munsee" (Muncie); they were severely slowed by weather.[32]

On November 8, 1831, the remainder of the community boarded the steamship *Ben Franklin* and headed for Saint Louis, where they hoped to rendezvous with the land party and, from there, to complete the journey to Indian Territory by wagon train as one group.[33] The boat party numbered about 230 individuals and included all of the headmen who had signed the 1831 treaty except Small Cloud Spicer, who had left in September.

The boat party arrived in St. Louis on November 16 with subagent Brish. Upon their arrival they discovered that the land party was ". . . stuck in snow and starving . . ." somewhere near the White River in Indiana. Most of their horses had died and they were out of provisions, with supplies difficult to obtain due to their distance from settlements and the severe weather. Clark reported in December 1831 "the Indians being frost bitten, sick and some dying and the whole party being much discouraged." Among the first to die among the land party were headman Wipingstick's youngest child and Cayuga James's oldest child.[34]

Sometime between November 16 and the end of December, subagent Brish set off to locate the land party and bring them to St. Louis.[35] It appears, however, that Brish simply returned to Ohio for the winter and was relieved of his duties until March of 1832, when he was reinstated by Superintendent Clark.[36] The land party spent the winter camped south of "Munseytown," supported by local settlers, charity groups, and their interpreter, Martin Lane, who drew on his personal finances. Resources were further stretched when thirty Delaware joined their camp in December. Because the Delaware had yet to sign an agreement for removal, resources could not be distributed to them from the government; however, the Sandusky community supported their needs and agreed to see them to Indian Territory.[37]

The details of the removal for both the land party and the entire community's walk from St. Louis only came to light two years after the Sandusky people's departure when in late summer 1833 the U.S. Treasury auditor, W. B. Lewis, sought an explanation for cost overages, stating: "The party conducted by you moved forward at the rate of only about six miles per day, whereas . . . all the other emigrating parties of Indians travelled at a rate at least double that each day." He also questioned the cost of what little provisions were given to either party.[38]

The Treasury auditor's investigation into the slow rate of travel as well as expenditures nearly double the originally estimated cost generated a flurry of responses and supporting documentation from Superintendent William Clark and subagent Brish. Clark's detailed letters responding to the auditor present us with a description of a confused and disorganized spectacle of human translocation. Indian Affairs had distributed the treaty annuities and cash due the Sandusky people prior to their departure, making the Piqua agents responsible for transporting nearly a year's worth of food rations, supplies, farm implements, and some livestock for the entire community from Sandusky to Indian Territory. Many Sandusky peoples had taken annuity funds and purchased items prior to leaving the reservation, and brought with them all of their furniture, stoves, and other household items. Some of the oldest and most infirm community members chose to travel by land, which required additional wagons. The scene described by Clark involved a train of at least thirty wagons, forty horses, and several tons of supplies for the land party alone.[39]

After arriving in St. Louis, Brish attempted to move the boat party onward to Indian Territory; however, the train of eighteen wagons and the 230 people on foot and horseback almost immediately became bogged down in heavy snow and freezing temperatures north of St. Louis. Subagent Brish, who accompanied his charges on horseback, wrote Clark in December 1831:

> I started with the Seneca Indians under my charge, but in consequence of the extreme coldness of the weather progressed but slowly upon our journey. On our arrival at St. Charles a considerable number were found to be too unwell to be moved further, and one woman died, fourteen were left. With the residue I continued my journey to within four or five miles of Troy, there two others died, and nearly the whole number became more or less unwell; a number of the children had their feet and hands frozen. Finding ultimately that we could proceed no further, I pitched an encampment on Quiver Creek until a suitable time for the journey shall arrive.[40]

The boat party remained encamped at Troy, fifty miles from William Clark's headquarters in St. Louis, until May of 1832. While at Troy, the community built temporary wood houses and lived in tents. They began to starve as they consumed the majority of their supplies or lost rations to wetness, rot, and raids by local Indians. Agent McElvain did not obtain the supplies needed before departure, such as the blankets and rifles that were to have been transported to St. Louis by the land party.[41] The Wyandotte on their return from exploring proposed new lands in Indian Territory passed through the land party's encampment in Indiana and reported the sad state of the people to Gardiner. Things at the Troy camp did not improve either despite Clark securing a contract with a local to provide daily rations, rifles, blankets, and horses. Between

December and April the Troy encampment saw the death of Mohawk Chief Charlieu, at least ten other adults, and an unspecified number of children, all of whom were buried at the encampment. Both Superintendent Clark and Gardiner were becoming increasingly concerned about both groups of Sandusky people turning back and attempting to resettle in Ohio.[42]

By March of 1832 Brish had been reinstated by Superintendent Clark and instructed to "collect" the people camped in Indiana and proceed with them to the Troy camp and then onto Indian Territory.[43] Brish arrived at the Munseetown camp in early April and began moving the land party along with the thirty or so Delaware toward St. Louis.[44] Arriving at the Troy camp in late April, Brish found the water party in a dissolute state and estimated the number of sick and dying at nearly one hundred. The rains and melting snow of spring 1832 continued to make the Quiver River near Troy too high for crossing the wagon teams and the travelers. The whole group was required to move up river to locate a boat to take them across in groups over multiple days. As the community began preparations for departure, they were required to leave six extremely ill and dying people in their winter "wigwams" to survive as long as possible on their own. Another sixteen people were too ill to travel by horseback or foot and waited at the Troy camp for wagons to transport them.[45]

On May 8, only fifteen days after they finally departed Troy, measles broke out among the Sandusky children near Jefferson, Missouri. The group kept traveling, covering only 250 miles in thirty days and arriving at Marais des Cygnes near Harmony Mission on June 12. High water and muddy roads forced the group to camp for another week nearby. While camped, many of the children and a few elderly women succumbed to measles and were buried at the mission.[46] Brish's next communication with Clark was on July 16, 1832, announcing the arrival of the "emigrant Senecas from Sandusky on the lands assigned to them."[47] In this final letter one year before his resignation, Brish laments:

> I charge myself with cruelty in forcing these unfortunate people on at a time when a few days' delay might have prevented some deaths, and rendered the sickness of others more light, and have to regret this part of my duty, which, together with the extreme exposure to which I have been subjected, and the sickness consequent upon it, has made the task of removing the Senecas excessively unpleasant to me.[48]

Brish's sympathy and care for the emigrant Seneca were short-lived. He resigned from his post shortly after arriving in Indian Territory despite having signed a contract to be Seneca agent for an additional year. The difficulties of removal weighed heavy on agents and new emigrants alike as tensions flared between populations indigenous to the area, such as the Osage, and newly removed peoples. Besides being displaced, the majority of the people occupying what is today the border areas shared by Missouri, Oklahoma, Kansas, and Arkansas were under the constant threat of violence. The Sandusky people, however, seemed to deal with their new challenges in the same way they always had: seeking clear-mindedness and autonomy.

FIVE

REFUSING FRAGMENTATION

Not a year after removal, the emigrating Seneca again found themselves in council with Indian agents. President Jackson, it seems, was concerned about the continued use of ancient forms of social and political organization among the newly removed peoples. The majority of the peoples removed from Ohio, Indiana, and Illinois continued to function according to the council system, mostly influenced by a significant commitment to traditional religions, unlike the Six Nations, who all had some form of centralized government coexistent with ancient forms of social organization and some forms of syncretism with Christianity. Indian Territory was becoming increasingly messy, with conflicts between communities as well as divisiveness over annuity distribution and land boundaries.[1]

To address these problems, President Jackson and Congress appointed, in July of 1832, former North Carolina congressman and governor Montfort Stokes to head a three-person commission. In 1833 Stokes, Henry L. Ellsworth of Connecticut, and John F. Schermerhorn of New York established their headquarters at Fort Gibson in present-day Muskogee County, Oklahoma. They brought with them three companies of mounted rangers, who were to provide pacification for hostile Western tribes. The Osage, Comanche, Kiowa, and Wichita were increasingly hostile to both settlers and new removed peoples. Stokes was charged with containing violence as well as persuading these communities to agree to terms under treaties. Additionally, Stokes was authorized to consolidate communities with shared geographic and cultural origins into single social and political units.[2]

Ronald Satz has interpreted the desire to reunite emigrated peoples according to their familial, political, and cultural relations as an attempt to create tribal monoliths in Indian Territory for the ease of negotiations and political engagement. Out of these political and geographic consolidations of peoples with shared "consanguinity and manners," we see groups in Indian Territory merging the political structure of multiple autonomous towns as well as absorbing smaller communities into more broadly defined regional administrative units and emerging national governments. Creating more condensed social units would also provide more land for future nonnative settlement or for new Indian removals.[3]

No doubt the multiple divisions of societies into clans, towns, and factions, which were merged into a racial and national homogeneity in the mind of the settler state, caused problems for centralization. As Cass stated, "The tribes should not be broken into fragments, but that portions of each should be brought together." The intersocietal fragments represented by clans, moieties, ceremonial grounds, longhouses, and the like were the fundamental social institutions of the removed peoples, particularly the communities that maintained a commitment to cultural conservatism. As I have argued throughout, the maintenance of Great Law principles supported Seneca councils and ceremonial organization, which provided the fundamental cultural apparatus for community maintenance. It also contained an inherent autonomy challenging the hegemony of colonial administration—an autonomy seen throughout Seneca interactions with the settler state. Decision-making through the council system, which most people removed from the Midwest continued to use until the mid-twentieth century, maintained a sociopolitical cohesion and a level of autonomy amid the pressure to consolidate and civilize. Even during times of intracommunity conflict and external pressures, a deliberate approach inspired by the logic of the Longhouse prevailed and prevented a complete transition to settlement—something not unnoticed by colonial administrators.

Cass, in his report to the president on the activities of 1832, posits political and geographic centralization as a process to further distinguish between settler-oriented natives and cultural conservative natives within the same communities. He tells the president and Congress, "A few individuals, almost always half breeds and their connexions [sic], engrossing the intelligence and means of each of these small communities, may become assimilated to our institutions and eventually planted among us with safety. But this should never be permitted at the sacrifice of more important interests, and to the utter disregard of the fate, which awaits the unfortunate mass of these tribes, persuaded, or almost compelled to remain where they must rapidly decline, and at length disappear. Their progress is onward; and, regret them, as we may and must, no human power can arrest their march, or avert their consequences."[5]

Centralization also served to integrate societies based on settler-derived categories but also to disrupt kin-based commitments to community cultural logics. For Cass the "children of nature" who continue to adhere to traditional practices and sociopolitical organization should be separated by land and representation from those who seek the way of life of the settler and are willing to give up their "primitive right."[6] The notion of "primitive right" reflects the representational habits found in the interaction between colonizer and colonized, which remains distinct from the essential aspects of community sociocultural practice or the practices of what I previously defined as the "inner." After removal the "outside"—relations between the native and the settler state—slowly ceases to reflect the "inner" and also becomes the realm of modern indigenous nation-building.[7] In the post-removal era, political centralization sought to begin the fragmentation of colonial political engagement away from the practices of the "inner" for all communities. Attempts to remove colonial administration from the realm of the council house became only partially successful. The deliberation of the council continued to determine the course of community decision-making for the Seneca. The Seneca in question here were not inspired to maintain sociocultural practices by their engagement with the settler or as resistance. Rather, it was the continued use of logics of the Longhouse that allowed for survival, despite the best efforts of the Stokes Commission and the century of continuity-challenging legislation that would follow.

There are other possibilities for the analysis I have set out here in other eras of settled people's culture history. The activities surrounding removal provided the richest information for the Sandusky Seneca. However, over the course of the next one hundred years we see momentary flashes of attempts at clear-mindedness in community handling of critical issues. After removing to Indian Territory, the Sandusky community had many other decisions to make, such as amalgamating with the Lewistown Seneca, allowing schools into their community, problems with the flow of liquor into Indian Territory, and the devastating effects of the Civil War for Indian Territory. The documents of the Neosho tell of a community that mostly carried on the way it had in Ohio; as stated above, they took their cultural practices and went elsewhere. In these brief correspondences and reports we observe the overwhelming challenges faced by removed peoples, but we also see life carrying on. The people are farming, building houses and fences, and participating in the regional grain economy. They are also holding ceremony. Community members—under constant pressure to civilize and become more adapted to the ways of the settler—negotiated the colonial condition in the best way possible. If we were to view their lives, the social events, and any political controversy through the epistemological Iroquois, we end up using conceptual framework favoring culture change as assimilation, community deliberation as factionalism, and every social problem as a rupture in fundamental social institutions. However, when seeing the community as one thinking through the Longhouse, we instead find the same level of deliberation and adaptive approach to the incursion of settler society in the post-removal era.

Post-Removal Challenges to Autonomy

The charge of the Stokes commission was not only to consolidate peoples for ease of administration but also to help alienate cultural conservatives from others who were "willing to cultivate the arts of civilization." Cass's vision for the settler native was to "let the lands be apportioned among families and individuals in severalty, to be held by the same tenures by which we hold ours. . . . Assist them in forming a code of laws adapted to a state of civilization."[8]

The Stokes commission succeeded in consolidating the Sandusky people and the newly removed Mixed Band of Shawnee and Seneca previously of Lewistown, Ohio, in a treaty signed on December 29, 1832.[9] The treaty, signed by the same chiefs who negotiated the Sandusky removal, administratively changed the name of the Seneca of Sandusky and the Lewistown Seneca and Shawnee to the United Nation of Seneca and Shawnee. In this treaty, both groups ceded additional lands in Indian Territory and agreed to merge under a single governmental and economic system sharing annuities as well as gristmills and blacksmiths.[10]

Despite being administratively consolidated, the communities continued to maintain their sociopolitical autonomy, and the amalgamation of the two Seneca groups into a singular administrative structure seemed to not have the effect desired by the Stokes commission. Throughout the Neosho period, 1837–1874, the Sandusky people continued to be known as the as the "Seneca," "Emigrant Seneca," or the "Sandusky Seneca," while the Lewistown people were referred to as the "Mixed Band," "Seneca-Shawnee," or the "Lewistown Seneca and Shawnee." The Lewistown and Sandusky peoples occupied different areas of the Neosho reserve and the two groups maintained separate communities. From the correspondence of agents concerning annuities, decisions about schools, and other matters, the Sandusky people and Lewistown people had their own distinct and autonomous councils. In their dealings with the Neosho peoples, agents continued to distinguish between the "Mixed

Band" (Lewistown Seneca-Shawnee) and the Seneca (Sandusky Seneca) well into the 1860s, when a treaty was ratified by Congress splitting the Shawnee from the Seneca-Shawnee Mixed Band and further consolidating the Seneca portion of the Mixed Band geographically and administratively with the Sandusky Seneca.[11]

As the colonial administration continually sought a further narrowing of native political entities at Neosho, it also sought to reduce interactions with traditional forms government—an effort that appeared successful on paper, but was less so in reality for the communities and Indian agents. Realizing this as the case for most of the Indian Territory natives, colonial administrators locally and at the national level made civilization their post-removal preoccupation. The pressure to engage the settler economy and to educate young people in government or mission-run schools ushered in the Neosho Subagency era for the Quapaw, Seneca-Shawnee, and Sandusky Seneca.

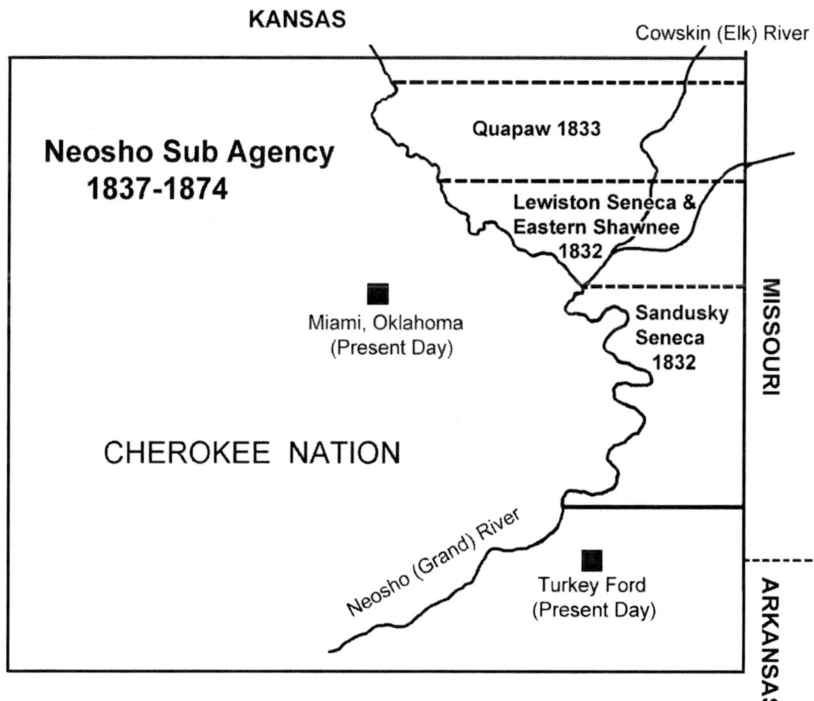

Figure 5.1 Neosho Sub-Agency. *Source:* Brian J. Gilley and Mary Connors

The era of the Neosho Subagency in Indian Territory began in 1837 with its headquarters on Sandusky Seneca lands. Not all colonial administrators saw removal and consolidation as ideal. Superintendent of the Western Territory William Armstrong expressed his skepticism about populating the frontier with natives and feared the possibility of cross-tribal alliances based on a shared hatred of the United States. Such a high concentration of peoples could be dangerous and would require a perpetual paternalism to ensure natives' dependency on the Great Father. He states in his report to the Commission of Indian Affairs in 1839:

> It has been seriously apprehended by many whose opinions are entitled to great consideration, whether or not concentrating so large a body of the aborigines upon our western border might not endanger the peace and prosperity of the frontier, especially as many of the emigrants have left their native land with great reluctance, and come over to the homes prepared for them in the west with embittered feelings. They are here contiguous to each other, and could soon unite and make themselves thereby more formidable to those whom they look upon as their oppressors. This feeling is more or less implanted in the bosom of every Indian to a white man. Thus far however well founded those fears were supposed to be, they happily have not been realized. Every Indian of common intelligence regardless of the feelings he may entertain of what is past, cannot but look forward and see that here is the last home left for the red man: beyond him, to the west, he is bounded by the vast prairies stretching onto the mountains. Heretofore, treaties have been made for their lands whenever their necessities seemed to require it, or the wants of the white brethren seemed to demand it. They are now removed beyond the limits of any state or territory, are exclusively under the control of the Government of the United States. Its plighted faith is given for the undisturbed possession the benefit of the different tribes arising from the proceeds of the sale of their lands. This policy gives them a common feeling with us in the perpetuity of our Government, as well as a strong inducement to refrain from everything calculated to disturb the peace of our citizens. Thus by pursing a steady, parental and soothing care over the different tribes they will be induced to look upon us, not as oppressors but as benefactors.[12]

Armstrong's comments reflect a quandary faced by the men in charge of overseeing the removed peoples at Neosho and Indian Territory in general. The minority seemed to support Armstrong's view of a paternal and dependent approach, as the majority was disturbed by the inconsistency of the Seneca and others in mastering the lifestyle of settlers. In contrast to Armstrong, the settler state was not interested in continuing what it saw as economic sponsorship of native communities. Being beneficiaries of civilization, not of economic patronage, was critical to converting the Neosho people into settlers and insuring their ability to be economically autonomous. The subsistence approach to life greatly frustrated the Protestant settler work ethic of the agents, who saw land and opportunity wasted by the idleness of Neosho peoples.

In the time between removal and the Civil War, the Seneca had used their gristmill and surplus grain to ensure the community was fed and all had what they needed.[13] When there were sufficient funds, food, and housing, the community entered a stasis where little agricultural was being done and even less was done to create a frontier capitalist infrastructure on the reserve. Around annuity time the community would purchase food, supplies, and household goods from authorized traders and try to make them last until the next distribution.

Observations of the Seneca's subsistence lifestyle among agents and superintendents emphasize their economic strategies as indolent and overtly resistant to civilization. Through settler logics agents tell a one-dimensional story of a community struggling with the ability to become civilized and equally resistant to their obvious need to transform themselves into full-scale agriculturalists. Neosho subagent John B. Luce writes in 1841:

> They appear to be decidedly retrograding; many houses are going to ruin, fences tumbling down and farms once flourishing, overgrown with weeds. The cause of all this said a curious instance of the evil that may result from schemes, apparently judicious, for the improvement of the Indians. Before removing to their present location, being already pretty well advanced in agriculture, they were promised as an inducement to further exertion, a grist and saw mill. The mills were built; but unfortunately there were no others in that part of the country. Consequently, the white settlers from adjoining counties in Missouri and Arkansas flocked in with grain and timber and the mills soon yielded a handsome revenue; the tolls of the grist-mill alone amounting,

in good season to nearly two quarts of meal per day to each individual of the tribe—double the ordinary flour ration allowed to privates in the army. Many an industrious and well disposed Indian has been induced, first to give up labor, as necessary, and next to sell his surplus meal for whiskey.[14]

Settler accounts such as this are often taken as a description of a community in decline or one in a constant state of struggle for survival in the white man's world. The contradiction between settler and native cultures is thought to put the Indian at a disadvantage in the relationship with more powerful state-sponsored national frontierism. Thus we are to believe the Indian is left with only a choice between the settler lifestyle and "traditional" tribal culture.

The agents' disappointment does tell us about the incompatibility between Seneca sociocultural and economic autonomy and settler understandings of a proper existence. However, we can alternatively read settler disappointment as the Sandusky Seneca extending community cultural logics to new circumstances and opportunities. Through settler logic, the sporadic nature of Seneca planting and harvesting for surplus is indolence, laziness, and a childish resistance to civilization. Yet Seneca reluctance to plant and harvest on settler cycles is neither a failure on their part nor a weapon of the weak. Rather it is an extension of community cultural logics to the conditions of the Neosho reservation. For example, the gristmill and all that it provides is brought into the sociocultural practices of the community, rather than the fabric of the community being transformed by the use of the mill. The income provided by the gristmill, to the disappointment of the colonial administration, does not become a vehicle for transforming the Seneca into frontier capitalists. Rather it becomes another extension of already existing and culturally durable socioeconomic practices.

Providing milling services for surrounding native farmers and settlers as well as annual annuities allowed for economic autonomy and reduced the need for large surplus-oriented agriculture. The combination of hunting, government-provided resources, food grown in home gardens, and income from the use of the gristmill provided for a sustainable existence. The agents' frustration tells us that the Seneca were continuing to live as they had in Ohio centuries before: by community standards emanating from a sociocultural autonomy. We do not see a community outwardly resisting the demands of the settler state, nor do we see the "indolence" and desperateness portrayed by agents. Rather we see a community living according to values incompatible with the colonial administration's rush to transform natives into settlers and expand the economic viability of the frontier. Agent reports tell the story of a community working diligently on a seasonal basis and engaging in economically productive activity as needed. It also tells a story of self-directed change through a set of locally defined social values.[15]

In addition to the sporadic nature of the community's "progress" toward agricultural and economic civilization, agents were frustrated by the resistance to schools on the part of the Sandusky Seneca as well as the Seneca and Shawnee Mixed Band.[16] Neosho subagent Barker noted in 1844: "The remaining two tribes of this agency (the Sandusky Seneca and the Mixed Band of Senecas and Shawnees) do not, as a tribe, feel much interest as yet in the subject of education; nor do they wish for the establishment of missions among them, although I have repeatedly in council brought the subject before them and recommended its adoption in the strongest terms. I am happy to be enabled to say that a few of the leading men of each tribe are in favor of schools." Yet he also notes that some Seneca chiefs have "anxieties" about having their children educated in schools.[17] In 1845, subagent James S. Raines, clearly critical of the Seneca reluctance to allow schools or missions on their land, praises the Quapaw, also Neosho Subagency peoples, in the same report, for their temperance and their supposed desire "to be educated by white men."[18] Reluctance for schools among the Sandusky Seneca and the Mixed Seneca-Shawnee Band was waning, according to Neosho subagent Andrew Dorn, by 1849. Dorn noted that many headmen had committed to sending their children to schools if they were established within the community, which did not happen until 1872, when agent Hiram Jones oversaw the construction of a school building and boarding house. Even then, very few Neosho Seneca attended.[19]

Beyond the pressure to send their children to settler-run schools, life alongside settlers had additional difficulties, William Armstrong, acting superintendent for the Western Territories, reported in 1839: "They live in log cabins; their residence is so close to the Missouri line, where whiskey can be so easily procured, that the Senecas have become much addicted to drinking spirits; the natural consequence is that they are becoming indolent."[20] Two years later, Armstrong again noted: "Their country is rich, healthy, and finely watered. They are however, so near the Missouri line, where spirituous liquor can be so easily obtained, that every inducement [is] held out to them by establishing whiskey shops for their accommodation. All these temptations are not easily resisted by Indians and prove their greatest curse."[21]

The cross-border trade in whiskey had a significant impact on the native communities along the Missouri border, as Osage subagent Calloway noted in 1843: "I am told (and I confidently believe it true) that the Osages have, within the last twelve or fifteen months, drunk more whiskey than they had done since they were a people. Upon our southeast border, or rather east of the Seneca (60 or 70 miles distant,) is a large steam distillery able to make from five to seven barrels a day. This house furnishes (I have not doubt) at least one hundred retailers to Indians. A majority of the houses immediately on and near the line . . . keep whiskey to sell the Osages for their money, their ponies, their rifle guns and their buffalo robes and blankets."[22]

The Sandusky Seneca had themselves been drawn into the alcohol-bartering system as noted by subagent Barker in 1843: "The Seneca mills are erected below, upon the same creek with one of these distilleries . . . they had a ready facility of procuring whiskey, for I have been told that they could get it in exchange for corn; and as they were entitled to the toll of their mill, some of them would take their proportion (which was much needed by their families at home,) and barter it for whiskey. The regulations of the mill are now such, that they are forced to abandon that practice entirely which has aided greatly the advancement of temperance and sobriety among them."[23] Barker further noted that Sandusky headmen George Curly Eyes and Small Cloud Spicer had been integral in the promotion of temperance among their people.[24]

In addition to extensive alcohol problems, the Sandusky Seneca were experiencing, according to agents, a population decline of about five percent per year. As noted by Superintendent Armstrong in 1844, "The Senecas from Sandusky, ten years ago, shortly after their emigration, numbered 250, now, there are but 125 of them. For this decrease . . . there is no perceptible cause."[25] Later in this same report Barker notes the year of 1844 as one of the most "sober" he has yet to observe since becoming an agent at Neosho.[26] Subagent James noted in 1847 that Seneca "chiefs" were "in full council, to their nation" advising their communities to stay away from liquor and beginning to establish temperance societies within the Neosho Agency. In 1850, the Sandusky Seneca, according to subagent Andrew Dorn, had established a temperance league, which was apparently making a positive impact.[27]

The Sandusky Seneca and the Seneca-Shawnee band often suffered in agent accounts by comparison with the more "civilized" Quapaw, who were portrayed as being in the forefront of native assimilation, education, and agricultural industry. In 1851, W. J. J. Morrow took over as Neosho subagent from Andrew Dorn and painted a very different picture of both the Quapaw and the two Seneca groups. Morrow claims both the Seneca groups, while being resistant to schools and assimilation, "drink less liquor than any Indians I am acquainted with." He further had strong words of reprimand for the Quapaw: "They have not made rapid advancement in civilization which many of the reports that have emanated from this office would indicate."[28] Morrow goes on to question the great strides in education and Christianity made by the Methodist church and Crawford Seminary established among the Neosho Quapaw in the late 1830s. Further, he noted, no Quapaw children appeared for school in the fall of 1851, and the seminary closed in February of 1852. The effect of the closing of the school, in Morrow's assessment, was the return of the natives to "their original habits, and [they] are now as wild and untamed as though they had never been within the classic walls of the Crawford Seminary."[29]

Agent descriptions of the character and problems among the Sandusky community give us only a glimpse of the lives of the actual people. What comes through, however, are the challenges created by the full assault on Sandusky Seneca social, religious, and political autonomy by settlers and colonial administration. The challenge to community autonomy created by alcohol, conniving settlers, and inconsistent agents, however, appears to have not affected the ability of the community to maintain socioreligious practices. Neosho subagent B. A. James noted in 1849:

> They have their regular dances, which they say is intended as an offering to the 'Great Spirit' for his kindness to them. About the 20th of August they have a yearly festival, or corn dance, in which the whole nation assembles at the council house. They bring with them all kinds of produce raised during the year; the women cook it. They will dance for two or three days and spend their time in eating and dancing, for the purpose of returning thanks to the 'great spirit' for a plentiful harvest.[30]

In his 1852 report Morrow described the Midwinter, within the same paragraph as that noting both Seneca communities' resistance to schools and missionaries:

> They adhere to many of their ancient customs, and partake of as few of the habits and manners of the white people as possible.

They have their festivals and various kinds of dances, at which they generally all attend. Their dog-dance comes off the first full moon in each year, and continues about one week. At this dance they sacrifice a white dog. He is gaudily dressed with different colored ribbons and hung by the neck to a gallows erected for that purpose. He remains hanging in this situation for three days; he is taken down and burned, and his ashes scattered to the four winds. They imagine that he goes to the spirit country, and is commissioned by the [sic] to bear such news as they wish communicated to their deceased friends and relatives. The ceremony is conducted with great solemnity, and all appear to be deeply impressed with its reality.[31]

Morrow's description of the "dog dance" reads as a testament to the continuity of community socioreligious practice some twenty years after the last dog dance at Sandusky and removal. Two brief mentions of ceremonial life in agent accounts will not satisfy the epistemological desires of particularists. However, the documentation of community gatherings at a minimum supports the argument for continued use of longhouse practices. The extent to which the Great Law was followed by the entire community is unknown, but again Morrow's descriptions bear an overwhelming resemblance to those of twenty years before. Agent accounts also tell us that the Neosho Seneca were practicing their religion, and holding council, while simultaneously resisting schools, turning away missionaries, and refusing a full conversion to settler agrarian capitalism.

Dealings with the settler state were not the only challenges to Seneca autonomy in Indian Territory. In 1843, the Neosho peoples, increasingly intermarried across communities and with other Indian Territory people such as the Cherokee, were drawn into a thirty-year-long dispute between the New York Cayuga and the Cayuga in Indian Territory, both of whom had inherited rights to eighteenth-century treaty annuities. The debate surrounded annuities due to the New York Cayuga by 1789 and 1795 land cession treaties with the state of New York.

When a group of Cayuga moved to Sandusky in 1807, they took with them rights to a portion of a $2,300 annual annuity due to the Cayuga residing in Canada, Ohio, and Cattaraugus. The Cayuga who became part of the Sandusky community, signed the 1831 treaty as Sandusky Seneca, and removed with them to Indian Territory had a claim to part of the annuity in question. "Chief of the New York Cayuga" Peter Wilson wrote New York Governor William Bouck in 1843 requesting that the Cayuga who moved to Sandusky and signed the 1831 removal treaty not be allowed to draw the annuity from the New York treaties. Payments were distributed only to individuals granted annuities under the original New York treaties and their descendants. At question for Chief Wilson was whether or not these descendants who were not part of the Cayuga Nation at Cattaraugus had continued claim to annuities.

Simultaneous to Chief Wilson's objections over Western Cayuga receiving annuities, a group of Cattaraugus Cayuga was in negotiations with Indian agents with the hope of removing to a reserve within the Osage Agency in Kansas. Wilson was also against the possibility of these potential emigrants having claim to annuities after they removed.[32] The issue of who had rights to the annuities was complicated by the close relationship maintained between the Ohio Iroquois and the Six Nations during the Sandusky years and their continued association during the Neosho years. In 1846, in fulfillment of the 1838 Buffalo Creek Treaty, a group of 153 Iroquois, including forty-four Cayuga, moved from tribal lands in New York to the "New York Tract" in Kansas. In 1847, Chief Wilson visited the New York Tract and continued the established pattern of migration by bringing a portion of the 1846 emigrant Cayuga and a portion of the Neosho Cayuga descendants back to Cattaraugus. After three years in Kansas, the remaining emigrant Cayuga moved to Neosho and joined the Neosho Seneca.[33]

The post-removal Cayuga migrations between Cattaraugus, Kansas, and Neosho, and back, extended kin relationships and rights to annuities across geographic and sociopolitical divides. In their ongoing claims against Western communities, the New York Cayuga argued that all the emigrant Cayuga now living at the Neosho Subagency no longer had a claim to the annuity payments because "the Cayugas residing with the Senecas have amalgamated with that people, so that it would be impossible to remove the Cayugas from the Senecas without breaking up families."

Chief Wilson himself recognized the complexity of national identity superimposed on traditional kin relations; he, however, weaved a story of false claims to the annuities by Cayuga living among the Neosho Seneca, about whom he wrote Governor Bouck: "The danger of being deprived of our just rights by false representations from our people of the Emigrating party and some of the Whites with whom they are allied and who are none too honest, makes our minds weary."[34]

The documents do not tell us if action was taken to deny annuities to the Cayuga living at Neosho, but the controversy appeared again in

1857 when a group of Cayuga headmen traveled to Cattaraugus Reservation to attempt to negotiate an "amicable adjustment." The Neosho chiefs representing Western Cayuga interests write: "We are accused of by the Cayugas of the East that we make a Fraudelent returns in taking Census of our people for the distiribution of our annuities due us from the State of New York it is alleged in their complaint that we have included people of other tribes in the enumeration."[35]

After arriving at Cattaraugus from Indian Territory, Western "Cayuga Chief" John Winney and Western "Seneca Chiefs" John Spicer and Isaac Warrior called a council with the New York Seneca in the hope they would act as arbitrators between the two parties. The resolution passed by the Cattaraugus Seneca council recommended that the disputing communities follow the stipulations of the treaty. However, the Cattaraugus Cayuga refused to abide by the decision of the Seneca Council and the three chiefs returned to Indian Territory without a resolution of the disagreement.[36] The dispute was finally settled by the New York State legislature, which passed a law directing the annuity to be divided per capita between the Western and New York Cayuga.[37]

After twenty years of dividing the annuities according to New York law, the controversy again emerged in 1875, when the New York Cayuga asserted that the Western Cayuga no longer used matrilineal kinship to determine Cayuga affiliation and thus should provide only an accounting of their numbers according to the mother's line. Indian agent H. W. Jones confirmed the community's use of bilateral Cayuga lineages for purposes of the per capita annuities. In 1875, the New York Cayuga took their grievance to the Comptroller of New York, to whom they claimed there would not be more than thirty Cayuga in Indian Territory if counted by matrilineage, compared to to the 154 claimed by the Neosho Cayuga.

It is unclear whether it was decided by council, but it appears as though both sides reached an agreement, and in 1876 the New York Cayuga began enumerating themselves by bilateral kin, making the number of eligible individuals 374. The comptroller did not agree with this new enumeration because annuity funds, he feared, were being used by other tribes with whom the Western Cayuga affiliated. The annuity argument ended here until the mid-1950s, when a claim to the annuities emerged within the federally recognized tribe among the descendants of the original emigrant Cayuga.[38]

Sorting out the independent relationship of certain Sandusky Cayuga descendants and newly emigrated Cayuga with the Six Nations as well as the state of New York is difficult with the documentation.

Erminie Wheeler-Voegelin proposed that there were few Seneca among the Sandusky Seneca or the Neosho peoples, with the majority being Cayuga. She read the documentation as showing a stronger Cayuga presence as well as a Cayuga domination of the sociopolitical landscape at Sandusky and Neosho. However, when trying to understand the Cayuga debate about annuities, we again find ourselves with too little evidence and the vestiges of a perspective favoring fragmentation. What the evidence tells us, at the least, is that through time the Cayuga maintained a kin-based affiliation with some sense of a distinct Cayuga identity. We cannot know to what degree individuals saw themselves as solely Cayuga and separate from other peoples within the Neosho Seneca. Through the lens of the sociocultural history of the Iroquois, it would make complete sense for Cayuga descendants and newly emigrated Cayuga to be an autonomous kin group among a larger sociopolitical entity in the same way clans continued to be. What we cannot know, however, is whether this autonomous kin group of Cayuga was simply an administrative accounting of descendants for the eighteenth-century treaties or was a sense of separate identity supported by continued connection to other Cayuga people across space and time. As the Neosho peoples continually sought to solve community problems, they clearly continued to think through the Longhouse as this debate over annuities continued into the twentieth century and was again brought before tribal council.

Council subjectivity continued to play an important role in Seneca relationships with other communities in Indian Territory. The community's commitment to councils was exploited by the Cherokee and the newly formed Confederacy at the onset of the Civil War. The crisis of the Civil War in Indian Territory led to several multicommunity councils and to the Neosho peoples seeking shelter among the Ottawa in Kansas. Seeking native allies for the Confederacy, the secessionist Cherokee held a grand council in 1861, inviting every community in Eastern Territory to Tahlequah, the Cherokee Nation Capital. According to a Peoria known as Baptiste, the newly appointed commissioner of Indian Affairs for the Confederacy, Albert Pike, enlisted former Neosho subagent Dorn to notify his former charges that John Ross, chief of the Cherokee of Oklahoma, had called them to a council at the Cherokee Nation to hear proposals from the Confederacy. However, upon their arrival, it appeared to Baptiste that John Ross was being forced to represent the interests of Pike and other secessionists under threat of harm.[39]

The Seneca were uneasy about making an alliance with the Confederacy, but one month after the first council the Seneca and the Mixed

Seneca-Shawnee Band signed treaties with Pike on October 4, 1861. The Seneca treaty contained forty-three articles which vowed annuities and Confederate protection of the community and disallowed settlement on community lands. The treaty did not ally the Seneca militarily with the Confederacy, but did give the secessionist government wide latitude to build roads, forts, and outposts and use livestock and agricultural products.[40] The Confederacy paid the Seneca and the Mixed Band annuities one time, and within a year Confederate support of the Neosho peoples was over when war came to their agency. Stand Watie's Cherokee detachment barely escaped a routing from Union Colonel Charles Doubleday in June of 1862 at the Battle of Cowskin Prairie, about one hundred miles south of the Neosho Agency headquarters. The summer of 1862 saw other battles and Cherokee-Confederate defeats within Seneca territory along the Neosho in Locust Grove and Old Fort Wayne.[41]

By July of 1862 nearly all of the Neosho Seneca had fled to the Ottawa reserve in Kansas, where Neosho Agent Peter Elder had moved his headquarters to Fort Scott. As in times past, the Seneca relied on their close relationship with other communities to find respite from conflict and to share resources.[42] The Seneca along with other Neosho peoples established an encampment along the Marias de Cygnes River within the Ottawa reservation. A. V. Coffin, the directing physician in charge of the health of the Kansas refugees, noted in his 1863 report that:

> The diseases prevailing to the greatest extent among this people are purely gastric or gastro-enteric in their character, and the result of the irregularity in the amount of nutriment contained in any given measure of food supplied them. Excessive hunger is the result. . . . The type of disease second in importance is pneumonia. This results from exposure to atmosphereic vicissitudes, with but very inadequate protection by clothing, tents or other habitations. This type is, of all others, the most fatal to Indians, according to my observation.[43]

By the fall of 1863 the Neosho Agency was fully occupied and plundered by Confederate forces and the majority of able-bodied men among the Kansas refugees were fighting with the Union Army. The situation among the Kansas refugees was growing worse, and W. G. Coffin, superintendent for the Southern Superintendency, had to request funds to support the eighteen thousand refugee natives for an additional year with food, clothing, housing, and medicine.[44] Despite the shift in allegiance and supplying ten percent of the soldiers for the Kansas regiment, the federal government withheld annuities from the Neosho peoples, presumably because they had signed treaties with the Confederacy, which foreshadowed future sacrifices. The Neosho slowly began making their way back to Indian Territory in the spring of 1865.[45]

At war's end, not to lose an opportunity to obtain land, colonial administrators named all communities who originally signed a treaty with the Confederacy traitors and demanded land cessions and modifications to removal treaties as reparations. A board of commissioners, which included Ely S. Parker, Seneca headman and Civil War hero turned U.S. Government negotiator, was sent to Fort Smith, Arkansas, to renegotiate treaties with all of the communities that had treated with the Confederacy. On September 8, 1865, a council of delegates from most of the groups in Indian Territory assembled at Fort Smith. As Superintendent Coffin describes the council:

> Immediately upon the opening of proceedings, the tribes were informed generally of the object for which the commission had come to them; that they for the most part, as tribes, had, by violating their treaties—by making treaties with the so-called confederate states, forfeited all rights under them, and must be considered as at the mercy of the government; but that there was every disposition to treat them leniently, and above all a determination to recognize in a signal manner the loyalty of those who had fought upon the side of the government and endured great sufferings on its behalf.[46]

The delegates and the commission were in council for thirteen days, during which time many of the delegates held councils among themselves. The federal commission was pressuring delegates to cede lands, alter boundaries, and agree to modified forms of government. On the whole, the delegates refused such sweeping changes without taking the requests back to their communities for deliberation. Isaac Warrior, the delegate from the Neosho Seneca, spoke to the council, addressing Ely Parker specifically:

> And then this is the way we were served there and did it to save our lives. Our hearts were not in the business, but with the north. So we went home and the chiefs in council said we would see our Great Father and see his hands. As soon as we

see his hands we will get out and go to him. After that we saw our Grand Father's hands, and started right away to him, and when we got there, caught right hold of them. We told our agent (his name was Elder) we want our Grand Father to forgive us for these acts, and not to think hard; and we all think, we three tribes, we have never done anything contrary to the will of our Grand Father. Not one of our men, of these three tribes I mentioned before, went south; that shows we didn't do anything to our Grand Father, didn't even scratch him; and when we got to Kansas our young men went into the army and helped our Grand Father to fight; and here are our brothers, they have seen our men in the army, where I said they were. Last fall we had a council with the Sac Indians, and the agents and superintendents were all there and we told them we were all loyal and would stand up for our Father; that's the reason we thought we had done nothing contrary. What we did we could not help. Then we always thought when and after this war broke out, when we ran away we did nothing, and always consider the land we have as ours yet, and we want to stand there yet; and my fathers I tell you this plainly, the shortest I could, so you could understand, we want our Grand Father to understand we are on his side, and have not broken any new treaties, we have no power to make any, because our people didn't authorize us to do so. And about another thing, the negroes. We haven't anything to say about them, because we haven't any negroes in our nation. And another thing was laid before us, about setting apart some lands for other nations north, in Kansas, for instance. If they want to come and make a treaty with us, we are ready to do so, if we like what they say and our Grand Father would like it. This is all I have to say at present.[47]

Isaac Warrior was later to praise the clear-mindedness of the proceedings and acknowledge the happiness of making the treaty and "shaking hands anew" with colonial administrators. Renewing alliance and the comfort that comes with it is no doubt an extension of the Longhouse. However, the oratory of Warrior does not read as a mea culpa for signing with the secessionists. Rather, it represents what I long expected was going on throughout this community's engagement with the settler state; holding its ground through its own understanding of the circumstances of settlement. Publicly recognizing the federal government's failure to meet its obligation of protecting the people of Neosho was a way of rejecting subordination while opening the door for administrators to reaffirm their commitment to the safety and well-being of Indian Territory natives.

The commission did succeed in convincing the delegates of their commitment to native safety and the curtailment of encroachments. However, the commission did not succeed in obtaining from the delegates attending the council cessions as reparation for treason. In the end, the entire delegation signed what amounted to statements of loyalty to the United States, which also required the communities to name themselves as traitors. Delegates also agreed to hear the federal government's case for additional cessions and modifications to removal treaties predicated on their treasonous behavior.[48]

With the admission of wrongdoing, Indian Affairs then was able to coerce leaders from multiple Indian Territory communities as well as natives from Indiana to Washington, D.C., to attend councils on additional removals, cessions, and consolidation. In 1867, Seneca leaders George Spicer and John Mush found themselves in council with colonial administrators negotiating land cessions, consolidation with other Western Iroquois, and changes to annuity agreements. The treaty of February 23, 1867, required the Seneca to sign over twenty thousand acres of their original reservation for settlement as well as for the newly removed Piankasaw, Peoria, Kaskaskia, Wea, and Miami who had occupied Kansas. The greatest impact on community organization was the dissolution of the Seneca-Shawnee Mixed Band and the consolidation of all Seneca into one sociopolitical structure.

Beyond Fragments

In the remaining years of the nineteenth century, the Neosho Subagency was closed and the Seneca were placed within the Quapaw agency. Except for brief mentions in annual reports to the commissioner of Indian Affairs around allotment, we hear very little about the Seneca until the Indian Reorganization Act of 1937, when they become officially known as the Seneca-Cayuga of Oklahoma. Post-removal life brought significant changes to the social-cultural and political practices of the communities that lived in Indian Territory. Allotment and Oklahoma statehood created further opportunities for community self-directed change. Twentieth-century Indian policy substantially affected many of the smaller and lesser-known communities, which lost a great deal of their political voice and ability to shape their living conditions.

Yet in the 1950s James H. Howard and Velma Nieberding documented a thriving ceremonialism among the Seneca-Cayuga. They found a group of Iroquois who continued to give importance to community gathering as their decendants had in nineteenth-century Ohio and carried on the fundamentals of their historic socioreligious practices.

In 1956 Nieberding attended the Green Corn at Turkey Ford, the location of the community's open-sided "longhouse," the form of which was highly influenced by the ceremonial arbors of their Southeast neighbors. Turkey Ford is on the Cowskin River and is part of the area originally occupied by the Sandusky Seneca on the Neosho Reservation. According to locals, Turkey Ford, which continues to be the location today of community gatherings, is the space of the ceremonial grounds established after removal in the 1830s. Nieberding's 1956 description tells of a typical Iroquois Green Corn conducted within a moiety- and clan-based organization. Nieberding observed the headman Lewis Whitewing giving a prayer of thanksgiving, a tobacco invocation, and a confession dance. The ceremony proceeded with the peach seed game, naming of babies, and a feast. Her brief account reads like any other ethnographic recounting of an Iroquois ceremony among the New York communities.[49]

Howard, who spent more time with the community in 1959, describes a similar scene at a Green Corn held at Turkey Ford. In the same way they had in the early nineteenth century at Sandusky, the 1950s Seneca-Cayuga extended Longhouse values to their neighbors and enfolded other community practices into their own values, such as inviting other tribal communities and leaders from the region to attend their dances, speak, and share practices. The weeklong Green Corn described by Howard includes all the components of a typical Iroquois Green Corn with thanksgiving dances, confessions, and feasting. After the Green Corn rituals for the day, Shawnee and Creek visitors led evening stomp dances. The mornings and afternoons were used for Iroquois-specific Green Corn rituals such as the peach seed game. In Howard's description of the last day, after the Green Corn officially ended, the men of the community participated in a series of dances called the sun dance or rain dance, which is said to be a prayer for sun, rain, and the cure of disease.

The Seneca sun dance, not to be confused with the sun dance of plains cultures, is another dance of thanksgiving held for the welfare of the community. Howard's description of the Seneca dance at Turkey Ford reads in the same way as those observed by A. C. Parker in the early twentieth century among New York and Canadian Seneca.[50] In typical syncretic fashion, the effigy of the sun used in the Seneca sun dance was danced from the outdoor ritual space through the eastern door of the longhouse, where the community commenced a war dance in the style of the Osage or Ponca. In this dance, community members danced around a drum in a circle to ritually specified songs wearing the traditional straight dance, grass dance, and cloth regalia common among surrounding prairie-plains peoples.[51]

What Howard observed at Turkey Ford was both ancient Iroquois and syncretized through multitribal influences. Particularists might see this as an example of the post-removal watering down of essential practices needed to claim a distinct and essential link with Iroquois tradition. However, a perspective of continuity sees the incorporation of stomp dancing, war dancing, and arbor-style longhouses as "extending the rafters" to include the sociocultural changes brought on through their active engagement with settlement, intermarriage, and the ever-changing sociocultural context of Indian Country. The participants in the confession dance or thanksgiving dance being clothed, as described by Howard, in plains-style war dance regalia does not represent a turn away from Iroquois. Rather it is a turn toward socioreligious persistence through the extension of Iroquois meanings to new social, kin, and political circumstances. A war dance, or a contemporary stomp dance, in an open-sided longhouse would no doubt be unfamiliar to the Iroquois ancestors of the Seneca-Cayuga, but I would argue that the fundamental principles upon which it is organized would be recognizable.

The challenges faced by the Sandusky community when viewed through the perspective presented in this book illustrate the ways in which the people have attempted to preserve themselves and their society amidst the unrelenting and sustained pressure of settlement. Community problems such as alcohol and conflicts over annuities are often taken as indicators of "factionalism" or other destructive forces. However, when viewed through the Longhouse, we see these issues being dealt with in ways particular to the Sandusky Seneca and carried forward by their Neosho Seneca and Seneca-Cayuga descendants. There are hints, when taken cumulatively, of a society attempting to hold itself together and use cultural conservatism to engage the processes imposed by settlement.

Looking at the documentation of a community such as the Sandusky Seneca through a perspective seeking to represent the various ways the challenges of settlement fragment people from one another as well as from their traditions will inevitably produce images of discontinuity. As Daniel Heath Justice tells us, we need to shift away from the terms of cultural suicide toward "opening room for the return of those models of self-determination that speak to the survival and presence of indigenous peoples, not simply the durability of individuals of indigenous ancestry. Certainly to open that space, we have to uproot those rank ideologies of fragmentation that have defined us. . . ."[52] The cultural continuity of the Sandusky people serves as both a testament to the durability of cultural logics, and a critique of settler states and logics attempting to fragment people away from traditions, fragment forms of representation away from the realities of cultural conservative life, and create epistemological fragments through analysis. Connecting the multiple durable logics used by the Sandusky people prevents the misinterpretation of their social and cultural mobility as a form of discontinuity and allows us to more broadly conceive of Iroquoisness as a set of values finding its grounding through use rather than geographic placement. For example, removal, as distasteful as it was, through particular community logics, was quite possibly an extension of a long history of autonomous translocation seeking to preserve an orientation toward the undifferentiated social elements governed by the longhouse.

Parmenter's *The Edge of the Woods* again tells us that the "Deganawidah Epic establishes crucial protocols for the regulation and inspiration of Iroquois behavior. Building on notions of duality, complementarity, and reciprocity prevalent in the Creation Story, narratives of the League's formation promote the idea of the inherent transformative power of people to effect positive change through movement in space."[53]

The epic itself tells of a man named Deganawidah, or the Peacemaker, who lived among people who did not heed his message of peace. He left his own people and traveled among the Iroquois, who were constantly at war with one another. In his travels, preaching the message of peace, he persuaded Hiawatha to give up war and blood revenge for the inconsolable loss of his daughter. Deganawidah consoled Hiawatha and returned him to peace with calm words and the gift of three strings of beads, which cleared his eyes so that he could see clearly, opened his ears so he could hear, and cleared his throat so he could speak words of peace and clear-mindedness.[54]

Together Deganawidah and Hiawatha traveled, spreading the message of peace, and transformed the warrior Tadodaho by straightening his hate-twisted body and removing the snakes from his hair. These three individuals become the symbols of the transformative power of boundary crossing and their actions form the basis of the Condolence Ceremony and thus the basic philosophical basis for the League. The aspect of the Condolence Ceremony dealing with spatial transformation is the second step in a series of five known as The Edge of the Woods, where mourners kindle a fire outside their village and welcome condolers with a "requickening address" to acknowledge the difficulty of their journey and to restore them to clear-mindedness.

Parmenter again tells us, "Understanding the Edge of the Woods as part of an innovative cultural process of remaking, rather than as a restoration or perpetuation of past reality, enables a better grasp of spatial and temporal changes in Iroquois history. Such an approach also eludes the 'authenticity trap' (or the insistence on stable, even static Iroquois cultural practices)."[55]

Authenticity and the ways it is conflated to geographic space challenge our ability to see the ways movement and sociocultural change emanate from an ontological reality. It is in this ontological reality where we see a refusal of epistemological categories seeking to fragment the Ohio peoples away from sociocultural heritages. The transitions of the Sandusky Seneca, within the arguments presented here, become a way of preserving clear-mindedness and peace temporally and spatially.

As I have argued throughout this book, the cultural logic of clear-mindedness and peace produced a form of subjectivity with roots in the cultural logics of the Iroquois, but also subjectivity specific to the Sandusky community. This subjectivity manifested itself in a clear commitment to community maintenance through socioreligious activities such as the Midwinter, but also in the sociopolitical realm of the council. This analysis is explicitly skewed toward continuity, but not at the expense of recognition of change. The goal has been to illustrate the ways in which change is self-directed within the available cultural logics and practices. Change is thus not a challenge to autonomy but rather upholds autonomy, and through autonomy continuity is made possible. Therefore, our challenge for further scholarship in this region during the nineteenth century is to approach the communities from a perspective recognizing the ways in which indigenous subjectivity is a self-directed act seeking various forms of culturally specific autonomy.

Abbreviations Used in Notes

JR	Jesuit Relations
NA	National Archive
RCCCCC	Records of the Continental and Confederation Congresses and the Constitutional Convention
OIA	Office of Indian Affairs
RBIA	Records of the Bureau of Indian Affairs
RG	Record Group
M	Microform
R	Roll
F	Frame
LSLRMS	Letters Sent and Letters Received, Michigan Superintendency
OVGLEA	Ohio Valley-Great Lakes Ethnohistory Archive
PCC	Papers of the Continental Congress
LSRDW	Letters Sent and Received Department of War
USCSS	United States Congressional Serial Set
CSEI	Correspondence of the Subject of the Emigration of Indians
RCIAUS	Report of the Commissioner of Indian Affairs United States
RSSIA	Records of The Southern Superintendency of Indian Affairs

NOTES

NOTES TO PREFACE

1. Richard White, *The Middle Ground: Indians, Empires, and Republics in the Great Lakes Region, 1650–1815* (Cambridge: Cambridge University Press, 1991); Michael McConnell, *The Upper Ohio Valley and Its Peoples, 1724–1774* (Lincoln, NE: University of Nebraska Press, 1992); Jon Parmenter, *The Edge of the Woods: Iroquoia, 1534–1701* (East Lansing, MI: Michigan State University Press, 2010).

2. Laurence Hauptmann provides an extensive analysis of the political disagreements and intratribal rivalries among the Seneca-Cayuga in *Iroquois Struggle for Survival: World War II to Red Power* (Syracuse, NY: Syracuse University Press, 1986), 65–83.

NOTES TO INTRODUCTION

1. Francis Jennings, *The Ambiguous Iroquois Empire: The Covenant Chain Confederation of Indian Tribes with English Colonies from its Beginnings to the Lancaster Treaty of 1744* (New York: Norton, 1984), 17–19; Dean Snow, *The Iroquois* (New York, NY: Blackwell, 1994), 175–6.

2. Lesli J. Favor, *The Iroquois Constitution: A Primary Source Investigation of the Law of the Iroquois* (New York, NY: Rosen Publishing Group, 2003), 16; Donald Grinde, *The Iroquois and the Founding of the American Nation* (San Francisco, CA: Indian Historian Press, 1977); Donald Grinde, "Iroquoian Political Concept and the Genesis of American Government: Further Research and Contentions," *Northeast Indian Quarterly* 6, no. 4 (Winter 1989): 10–21.

3. Jennings, *Ambiguous Iroquois*, 17.

4. Daniel N. Moses, *The Promise of Progress: The Life and Work of Lewis Henry Morgan*, (Columbia, MO: University of Missouri Press, 2009), 6.

5. Paul van der Grijp, "Pioneer of untaught anthropology: Recontextualizing Lewis H. Morgan and His Kinship Perspective, Dialectical Anthropology

(1997) 22: 106, 114. Carl Resek, *Lewis Henry Morgan, American Scholar* (Chicago, IL: University of Chicago Press, 1960), 31.

6. Robert Wiebe, *The Search for Order: 1877–1920* (New York, NY: Hill & Wang, 1966).

7. Partha Chatterjee, *The Nation and its Fragments* (Princeton, NJ: Princeton University Press, 1993), 6.

8. Philip Deloria, *Playing Indian* (New Haven, CT: Yale University Press, 1998), 40.

9. John Kelly and Martha Kaplan, *Represented Communities: Fiji and World Decolonization* (Chicago, IL: University of Chicago Press, 2001), 6.

10. Audra Simpson, "On Ethnographic Refusal: Indigeneity, 'Voice' and Colonial Citizenship," *Junctures: The Journal for Thematic Dialogue* 9 (2007), 67–80.

11. Duane Champagne, *Social Change and Cultural Continuity among Native Nations* (Lanham, MD: Altamira, 2006), 32.

12. Dipesh Chakrabarty, "Postcoloniality and the Artifice of History: Who Speaks for 'Indian' Pasts?" *Representations* 37 (Winter 1992): 1–26.

13. Emer Nolan, "State of the Art: Joyce and Postcolonialism" in *Semicolonial Joyce*, ed. Derek Attridge and Marjorie Howes (Cambridge, UK: Cambridge University Press, 2000), 78.

14. Chatterjee, *Nation*, 236.

15. Annemarie A. Shimony, *Conservatism among the Iroquois at the Six Nations Reserve* (Syracuse, NY: Syracuse University Press, 1994); Snow, *The Iroquois*, xiii–xvi; Anthony F. C. Wallace, *The Death and Rebirth of the Seneca* (New York, NY: Vintage, 1972).

16. William Fenton, "Problems Arising from the Historic Northeastern Position of the Iroquois," in *Essays in Historical Anthropology of North America*, Smithsonian Miscellaneous Collections 100, ed. Julian H. Steward, (Washington, D.C.: Smithsonian Institution, 1940), 159–252.

17. William A. Starna and Robert E. Funk, "The Place of the In Situ Hypothesis in Iroquoian Archaeology." *Northeast Anthropology* 47 (1994): 45–7; Richard MacNeish, *Iroquois Pottery Types: A Technique for the Study of Iroquois Prehistory*, Anthropological Series 31, *National Museum of Cannonade Bulletin* 124 (1952).

18. Fenton, "Problems Arising," 199–200.

19. Yael Ben-zvi, "National Appropriations and Cultural Evolution: The Spatial and Temporal U.S. of Lewis Henry Morgan's Native America." *Canadian Review of American Studies* 33:3 (2003): 211–13.

20. Akhil Gupta and James Ferguson, "Culture, Power, Place: Ethnography at the End of an Era," in *Culture, Power, Place*, ed. Akhil Gupta and James Ferguson, (Durham, NC: Duke University Press, 1997), 9; J. D. Peters, "Seeing Bifocally: Media, Place, Culture," in *Culture, Power, Place*, ed. Akhil Gupta and James Ferguson, (Durham, NC: Duke University Press, 1997), 81–2.

21. James Clifton, *Being and Becoming Indian: Biographical Studies of North American Frontiers* (New York, NY: Dorsey Press, 1989), 3.

22. Fred Voget, "Anthropological Theory and Iroquois Ethnography," in *Extending the Rafters: Interdisciplinary Approaches to Iroquoian Studies*, ed. Michael Foster, Jack Campisi, and Marianne Mithun (Albany, NY: SUNY Press, 1984), 347–8; William Fenton, *American Indian and White Relations to 1830: Needs and Opportunities for Study* (Williamsburg, VA: Institute of Early American History and Culture, 1957), 4, 21.

23. Kurt A. Jordan, *The Seneca Restoration 1715–1754: An Iroquois Local Political Economy*, (Gainesville, FL: University Press of Florida), 15.

24. Richard White, *Middle Ground*, xxx.

25. Kurt Jordan, *Seneca Restoration*, 16.

26. Richard White, *Middle Ground*, x, xiii.

27. James Axtell, "Ethnohistory: An Historian's Viewpoint," *Ethnohistory* 26, no. 1 (1979), 5.

28. Sherry B. Ortner, *High Religion: A Cultural and Political History of Sherpa Buddhism* (Princeton, NJ: Princeton University Press), 12.

29. Morris Foster, *Being Comanche: The Social History of an American Indian Community* (Tucson, AZ: University of Arizona Press, 1991), 16.

30. Lisa Brooks, *The Common Pot: The Recovery of Native Space in the Northeast* (Minneapolis, MN: University of Minnesota Press, 2008), xxiii.

31. Tol Foster, "Of One Blood: An Argument for Relations and Regionality in Native American Literary Studies," in *Reasoning Together: The Native Critics Collective*, ed. Craig S. Womack, Daniel H. Justice, and Christopher B. Teuton (Norman, OK: University of Oklahoma Press, 2008), 267.

32. Zhang Xianqing, "The Discourse of 'Tartar': The Proto-Ethnographic Descriptions of Manchu by European Missionaries in 17th Century," *Academic Monthly* (China) 2 (2009): 1.

33. Tol Foster, "Of One Blood," 267.

NOTES TO CHAPTER ONE

1. Thomas S. Abler, *Chainbreaker: The Revolutionary War Memoirs of Governor Blacksnake* (Lincoln, NE: University of Nebraska Press, 1989); Thomas Abler and Elisabeth Tooker, "Seneca," in *Handbook of North American Indians*, Vol. 15, ed. Bruce Trigger (Washington, D.C.: Smithsonian Institution, 1978); Michael N. McConnell, "Peoples In Between: The Iroquois and the Ohio Indians, 1720–1768" in *Beyond the Covenant Chain* (Syracuse, NY: Syracuse University Press, 1987), 93–114; Michael N. McConnell, *A Country Between: The Upper Ohio Valley and Its Peoples, 1724–1774* (Lincoln, NE: University of Nebraska Press, 1992); Wallace, *Death and Rebirth*; Marian White et al. "Cayuga," in *Handbook of North American Indians*, Vol. 15, ed. Bruce Trigger (Washington, D.C.: Smithsonian Institution, 1978), 500–504.

2. McConnell, "Peoples in Between," 94.

3. Ibid, 95; Daniel Richter, *The Ordeal of the Longhouse: The Peoples of the Iroquois League in the Era of European Colonization* (Chapel Hill, NC: The

University of North Carolina Press, 1992), 191–213; Wallace, *Death and Rebirth*, 112–113.

4. McConnell, "Peoples in Between," 93.

5. McConnell, *Country Between*, 4, 15–20.

6. Wallace, *Death and Rebirth*, 112, 122.

7. Richard Aquila, *The Iroquois Restoration: Iroquois Diplomacy on the Colonial Frontier, 1701–1754* (Lincoln, NE: University of Nebraska Press, 1997), 194–5.

8. Wallace, *Death and Rebirth*, 113; Richter, *Ordeal*, 256; Abler, *Chainbreaker*, 34; Lois Mulkearn, *George Mercer Papers* (Pittsburgh, PA: University of Pittsburgh Press, 1954), 501. McConnell, *Country Between*, 21; Randolf Downes, *Council Fires on the Upper Ohio: A Narrative of Indian Affairs in the Upper Ohio Valley until 1795* (Pittsburgh, PA: University of Pittsburgh Press, 1940), 9.

9. Downes, *Council Fires on the Upper Ohio*, 74.

10. McConnell, *Country Between*, 21–33; McConnell, "Peoples in Between," 93–112.

11. McConnell, *Country Between*, 24.

12. Ibid, 30–31.

13. Robert Toupin, *Les Ecrits de Pierre Potier* (Ottawa, Canada: Le Presses de l'Universite d'Ottawa, 1996), 171, 197.

14. Ibid, 41–43,

15. P. Armand de le Richardie, letter to P. Pierre Potier, December 10, 1750, reprinted in *Les Ecrits de Pierre Potier*, 463.

16. Toupin, *Les Ecrits de Pierre Potier*, 171, 197.

17. McConnell, *Country Between*, 75.

18. David M. Stothers and Timothy J. Abel, "Vanished Beneath the Waves: The Lost History and Prehistory of Southwestern Lake Erie Coastal Marshes." *Archaeology of Eastern North America* 29 (2001): 36.

19. Ibid, 38–9; Charles Augustus Hanna, *The Wilderness Trail: Or, the Ventures and Adventures of the Pennsylvania Traders on the Allegheny Path*, Vol. 2 (New York, NY: GP Putnam and Sons, 1911), 177, 181, 188–9, 206, 209, 210, 279; James Smith, captive of the Delaware, documents staying at Sunyendeand for a period of time. He states that Sunyendeand "lay upon a small creek which empties into the mouth of the Sandusky." James Smith, *An account of the Remarkable Occurrences in the life and travels of Col. James Smith, During his Captivity with the Indians in the Years 1755–59* (Cincinnati, OH: Robert Clarke and Co., 1870), 50, 100–102.

20. David L. Preston, *The Texture of Contact: European and Indian Settler Communities on the Frontiers of Iroquoia, 1667–1783* (Lincoln, NE: University of Nebraska Press, 2009), 225.

21. Basil Meek, "Tarhe—The Crane," in Ohio Archaeological and Historical Collections, Volume 2, ed. Henry Howe (Columbus, OH: Fred Heer, 1911), 67; Emilius O. Randall, *The History of Ohio*, Vol. 2 (New York, NY: Century History Company, 1912), 561–564.

22. John Heckewelder, letter to Peter S. Du Ponceau, Bethlehem, PA, 12 August 1818, reprinted in *Ethnohistory* 6, no. 1, (1959), 72.

23. William Fenton, *The Great Law and the Longhouse: A Political History of the Iroquois Confederacy* (Lincoln, NE: University of Nebraska Press, 1998), 533–8; Siegrun Kaiser, "Munsee Social Networking and Political Encounters with the Moravian Church," ed. A. G. Roeber (University Park, PA: Pennsylvania State University Press 2008): 159.

24. Ibid, 582; R. Douglas Hurt, *The Ohio Frontier: Crucible of the Old Northwest, 1720–1830* (Bloomington, IN: Indiana University Press, 1996), 57, 59, 68; Reuben G. Thwaites and Louis P. Kellogg, *Documentary History of Dunmore's War, 1774* (Madison, WI: Wisconsin Historical Society, 1905), 304.

25. Clarence M. Burton, "Ephraim Douglas and His Times: A Fragment of History." *The Magazine of History*, No. 10 (1910), 41; Erminie Wheeler-Voegelin, "The 19th and 20th Century Ethnohistory of Various Groups of Cayuga Indians" (1959), Great Lakes Ohio Valley Ethnohistoric Project Archives, Indiana University Bloomington.

26. General R. Butler, letter to Major General Henry Knox, 20 March 1787, Records of the Continental and Confederation Congresses and the Constitutional Convention, Microform 247, 550, National Archive.

27. Ibid.; Major Wyllys, letter to Colonel Harmare, 6 February 1787, RCCCCC, Microform 247, 550, NA, Papers of the Continental Congress; Mr. Vonswearingen, letter to Col. W. Butler, 29 September 1787; R. Butler, letter to Maj. Gen. Knox, 11 October 1787.

28. Heckewelder, letter to Peter S. Du Ponceau, 72; *Treaties Between the United States and the Indian Tribes*, ed. Richard Peters (Boston, MA: Charles Little and James Brown Publishers, 1848), 54.

29. Charles Whittlesey, *Early history of Cleveland, Ohio, including original papers and other matter relating to the adjacent country. With biographical notes of the pioneers and surveyors* (Cleveland, OH: Fairbanks, Benedict & Co., Printers, 1867), 402.

30. Wheeler-Voegelin, "19th and 20th Century Ethnohistory", v–vii, 7, 14–15.

31. Ibid, 20; J. Johnston, letter to W. H. Crawford, Sec. of War, 6 June 1815, Office of Indian Affairs, Letters Sent and Received, Department of War, Microform 1, Roll 3, NA.

32. "Treaty with the Wyandot, Etc., 1814," in *Indian Affairs: Laws and Treaties, Vol. II, Treaties*, compiled and edited by Charles J. Kappler (Washington, D.C.: Government Printing Office, 1904).

33. A.J. Dallas, letter to Maj. Gen. W. H. Harrison, 9 June 1815; J. Johnston, letter to W. M. Crawford, 18 October 1815, Office of Indian Affairs, Letters Received and Sent, Department of War, Microform 1, Roll 2, NA.

34. J. Johnston, letter to unidentified person at Dept. of War, 12 June 1817, OIA, LRSDW, Microform 1, Roll 3, NA.

35. D. A. Ogden, letter to Gov. L. Cass, 13 June 1817, OIA, LRSDW, Microform 1, Roll 3, NA.

36. Charles Jouette, letter to J. C. Calhoun, 12 July 1817, OIA, LRSDW, Microform 1, Roll 3, NA.

37. E. Granges, letter to unknown person at War Department, 10 July 1817, OIA, LRSDW, Microform 1, Roll 3, NA.

38. Unknown, letter to General D. McArthur, 13 June 1817, OIA, LRSDW, Microform 1, Roll 3, NA.

39. Sturtevant, "Seneca-Cayuga," 539–40; Erminie Wheeler-Voegelin, "The 19th and 20th Century."

40. Ibid, 21–28.

41. William Lang, *History of Seneca County, from the Close of the Revolutionary War to July, 1880: Embracing Many Personal Sketches of Pioneers, Anecdotes, and Faithful Descriptions of Events Pertaining to the Organization of the County and Its Progress* (Springfield, OH: Transcript Press, 1880), 96.

42. Richard White, *Middle Ground*, 2.

43. Susan Miller, "Licensed Trafficking and Ethnogenetic Engineering," in *Natives and Academics: Researching and Writing about American Indians*, ed. Devon A. Mihesuah (Lincoln, NE: University of Nebraska Press, 1998), 102–4.

NOTES TO CHAPTER TWO

1. John McElvain, letter to Secretary of War, 15 November 1831, Letters Sent and Letters Received, Michigan Superintendency, Microform 234, Roll 669.

2. Kelley and Kaplan, *Represented Communities*, 4.

3. M. Foster, *Being Comanche*, 28–9.

4. Champagne, *Social Change*, 30.

5. Shimony, *Conservatism*, 35; Fenton, *Great Law*, 23–24; Fenton, "Northern Iroquois Culture Patterns," in *Handbook of North American Indians*, ed. William Sturtevant (Washington, D.C.: Smithsonian Institution, 1978) vol. 15, 296–321; Champagne, *Social Change*, 14–15.

6. Claude Lévi-Strauss, *Totemism*, Trans. Rodney Needham (Boston: Beacon Press, 1963), 89.

7. Craig Womack, "A Single Decade: Book-Length Native Literary Criticism Between 1986–1997," in *Reasoning Together: The Native Critics Collective*, ed. C. S. Womack, D. H. Justice, and C. B. Teuton (Norman, OK: University of Oklahoma Press, 2008), 66.

8. Isaac I. Dumond, "Speech of Isaac Dumond Before the Seneca Pioneer Association," in Lang, *History of Seneca*, 97.

9. Henry C. Brish, letter to Col. S. S. Hamilton, 8 September 1831, Letters Sent and Letters Received, Michigan Superintendency, Microform 234, Roll 669; Lang, *History of Seneca*, 100.

10. Nevin Otto Winter, *A History of Northwest Ohio: A Narrative Account of its Historical Progress and Development from the First European Exploration of the Maumee and Sandusky Valleys and the Adjacent Shores of Lake Erie, Down to the Present Time*, Volume 1 (New York, NY: The Lewis Publishing Company, 1917), 155; "Annual report of the Bureau of American Ethnology to the secretary of the Smithsonian Institution," Issue 18, Part 2, (1896): 732–3; *Memoirs of the*

Miami Valley, Volume 1, ed. John Calvin Hover et al. (Chicago, IL: Robert O. Law Company,1919), 281–2; Harry E. Stocker, *History of the Moravian mission among the Indians on the White River in Indiana*, (Bethlehem, PA: Times Publishing Co. Printers, 1917), 170–1; J. B. Gardiner, letter to Lewis Cass, New Lebanon, Ohio, 1 December 1831.

11. Lang, *History of Seneca*, 100.

12. Charles Chester Cole, *James B. Finley, Frontier Reformer* (Lexington, KY: University Press of Kentucky, 1994), 4.

13. The original Sydney Aurora article is unavailable, however Brish's account is excerpted in Butterfield's *History of Seneca County: containing a detailed narrative of the principal events that have occurred since its first settlement down to the present time; a history of the Indians that formerly resided within its limits; geographical descriptions, early customs, biographical sketches, &c., &c., with an introd., containing a brief history of the state, from the discovery of the Mississippi River down to the year 1817, to the whole of which is added an appendix, containing tabular views, &c* (Sandusky, OH: D. Campbell & Sons, 1848), 66–9.

14. We know that Between-the-Logs visited and studied with the Prophet Handsome Lake as well as Tenkswatawa, the Shawnee prophet and brother of Tecumseh, for one year each. See Nathan Bangs, *A History of the Methodist Episcopal Church, Volume III* (New York, NY: Phillips Lincoln, 1837), 508–10; Martin W. Walsh, "The 'Heathen Party': Methodist Observation of the Ohio Wyandot," *American Indian Quarterly* 16, No. 2 (Spring 1992): 189–211.

15. John O. Choules and Thomas Smith, *The Origin and History of Missions: A Record of the Voyages, Travels, Labors and Successes of the Various Missionaries, who have been sent forth by protestant societies and churches to evangelize the heathen party* (Boston, MA: Gould, Kendall and Lincoln, 1848), 507–514.

16. James B. Finley, *History of Wyandot Mission*, (Cincinnati, OH: The Methodist Book Concern, 1840), 174–5.

17. Ibid, 176–7.

18. Ibid, 177.

19. Ibid, 178.

20. Dumond's circa 1824 description of a ball game in Lang, *History of Seneca*, 96; Winter, *A History of Northwest Ohio*, 195–6; Norman Newell Hill, *1803. History of Knox County Ohio, Its Past and Present* (Mt. Vernon, OH: A. A. Graham and Company Publishers, 1881), 195–6; Elisabeth Tooker, *The Iroquois Ceremonial of Midwinter* (Syracuse, NY: Syracuse University Press, 1970), 26–7, 34.

21. Champagne, *Social Change*, 40.

22. Detailed descriptions of the Midwinter are not available for the entire period, and for some years there is only a mention that a "dog sacrifice" took place. It was recorded for the dates: 1819 by Sally Ingham, in Lang, *History of Seneca*, 123; 1820 by Isaac Dumond, in Lang, *History of Seneca*, 97; 1821 by James Finley, in *History of Wyandot*; 1831 by S. Crowell, in Lang, *History of Seneca*, 102; and also in 1831 by James Brish, in Butterfield, *History of Seneca*, 66–69.

23. Lang, *History of Seneca*, 96.

24. Champagne, *Social Change*, 40.

25. Dumond, "Speech of" in Lang, *History of Seneca*, 97; Tooker, *Iroquois Ceremonial*, 5–7; Fenton, *Great Law*, 113–117.

26. E. Tooker, *Iroquois Ceremonial*, 40–1; Dumond, in Lang, *Seneca County*, 98–100.

27. Dumond, "Speech of," in Lang, *History of Seneca*, 97.

28. E. Tooker, *Iroquois Ceremonial*, 40–1; The firing of guns by "Big Heads" is documented by settler observer Samuel Crowell, "Crowell's Contribution," in Lang, *History of Seneca*, 100–1.

29. These descriptions come from Abraham Baughman, *History of Seneca County, Ohio: A Narrative of its Historical Progress, Its People, and its Principal Interests, Vol. I* (New York, NY: Lewis Publishing Company, 1911), 22–7.

30. S. Crowell, "Crowell's Contribution," in Lang, *History of Seneca*, 100–1.

31. Ibid, 102.

32. Ibid.

33. Harold Blau, "Dream Guessing: A Comparative Analysis," *Ethnohistory* 10:3, (1963): 241; E. Tooker, *Iroquois Ceremonial*, 88–90.

34. H. Blau, "Dream Guessing," 245; E. Tooker, *Iroquois Ceremonial*, 100–1.

35. Ibid; Reuben Gold Thwaites, ed. *The Jesuit Relations and Allied Documents*, Vol. 17, (Cleveland, OH: The Burrows Brothers Company, 1898), 193.

36. Ibid, 104. Dumond, "Speech of . . ." in Lang's *History of Seneca*, 97; E. Tooker, "The Iroquois White Dog Sacrifice in the latter part of the Eighteenth Century," *Ethnohistory* 12, no. 2 (1965): 130; Sally Ingham, "Sketch of Sally Ingham," in Lang, *History of Seneca*, 124.

NOTES TO CHAPTER THREE

1. Sandusky Senecas, letter to John Johnston, 2 June 1824, Microform 234, Roll 669, Frames 401–3, Office of Indian Affairs, Letters Sent and Received, Department of War, NA.

2. Lang, *History of Seneca*, 95–6.

3. John Johnston, letter to J. C. Calhoun, 11 February 1824, Piqua Agency Papers, 1824–1830, Microform 234, Roll 669, Frame 271, Office of Indian Affairs, Letters Sent and Received, Department of War, NA.

4. Mark Rifkin, *Manifesting America: The Imperial Construction of U.S. National Space* (London, UK: Oxford University Press, 2009), 38.

5. Champagne, *Social Change*, 38.

6. Kelly and Kaplan, *Represented Communities*, 83.

7. Sturtevant, "Seneca-Cayuga," 539–540; Wheeler-Voegelin, *The Ethnohistory of Various*, 24–25.

8. Rifkin, *Manifesting America*, 42.

9. Champagne, *Social Change*, 38.

10. Denis Foley, "Iroquois Mourning and Condolence Installation Rituals: A Pattern of Social Integration and Continuity," in *Preserving Tradition and*

Understanding the Past: Papers from the Conference on Iroquois Research, 2001–2005, ed. Christine Sternberg Patrick, New York State Museum Record 1 (2010), The University of the State of New York, The State Education Department, Albany, NY, 25–30.

11. Parmenter, *Edge of Woods*, xliv–xlv; Fenton, *Great Law*, 29–31.

12. Richter, *Ordeal*, 40–1; Fenton, *Great Law*, 31.

13. Greg O'Brien, "The Conqueror Meets the Unconquered: Negotiating Cultural Boundaries on the Post-Revolutionary Southern Frontier," *The Journal of Southern History* 67, no. 1, (2001): 51–2.

14. G. Graham, letter to L. Cass, 23 March 1817, LSLRMS, Microform 1, Roll 3.

15. G. Graham, letter to L. Cass and D McArthur, 19 May 1817, LSLRMS, Microform 1, Roll 3.

16. W. H. Crawford, letter to D. McArthur, 6 April 1816; G. Graham, letter to L. Cass, 23 March 1817; G. Graham, letter to L. Cass, 17 April 1817; G. Graham, letter to L. Cass, 19 May 1817; G. Graham, letter to L. Cass and D. McArthur, 19 May 1817; L. Cass, letter to G. Graham, 3 July 1817; L. Cass and D. McArthur, letter to G. Graham, 29 September 1817.

17. J. C. Calhoun, letter to Unknown Recipient, 24 October 1821, SLRMS, Microform 1, Roll 2.

18. Francis Paul Prucha, *The Great Father: The United States Government and the American Indians* (Lincoln, NE: University of Nebraska Press, 1986), x, 63; O'Brien, "The Conqueror Meets," 52.

19. J. Johnston, letter to L McKenney, 30 September 1818, LSLRMS, Microform 1, Roll 3.

20. J. Johnston, letter to N. Boilvin, 9 April 1822, LSLRMS, Microform 1, Roll 3.

21. J. Johnston, letter to L. Cass, 23 October 1820, LSLRMS, Microform 1, Roll 7.

22. J. Johnston, letter to J.C. Calhoun, 29 March 1819, LSLRMS, Microform 1, Roll 3.

23. Crittenden, letter to Calhoun, 28 September 1823, Ohio Valley-Great Lakes Ethnohistory Archive.

24. Oneida Chiefs, letter to L. Cass, 12 August 1820; J. Biddle, letter to L. Cass, 29 June 1821; T. Hunt, letter to the Six Nations Delegation, 30 June 1821; C. Nobles, letter to Mr. Sergeant, 19 August 1822; Microform 1, Roll 5, Office of Indian Affairs, Letters Sent and Received, Department of War, NA.

25. W. Clark, letter to J. C. Calhoun, 5 September 1823, Ohio Valley-Great Lakes Ethnohistory Archive.

26. Ibid.

27. Gilbert J. Garraghan, "St. Regis Seminary—First Catholic Indian School," *The Catholic Historical Review* 4 (April 1918): 457–9; J. Johnston, letter to T. L. McKenney, 11 April 1825, Letters Sent and Letters Received, Michigan Superintendency, Microform 234, Roll 669, Frame 428; Clark, letter to J. C.

Calhoun, 5 September 1823, Ohio Valley-Great Lakes Ethnohistory Archive; Duane Huddleston, Sammie Rose, and Pat Wood, *Steamboats and Ferries on the White River* (Conway, AR: University of Central Arkansas Press, 1998), 5; Thomas McKenney and James Hall, *History of the Indian Tribes of North America* (Philadelphia, PA: D. Rice and Company, 1872,) 377–9.

28. W. Clark, letter to J. C. Calhoun, 5 September 1823, Ohio Valley-Great Lakes Ethnohistory Archive; Crittendon, letter to Calhoun, 28 September 1823, Ohio Valley-Great Lakes Ethnohistory Archive; Clark, letter to Calhoun, 15 September 1823, Ohio Valley-Great Lakes Ethnohistory Archive.

29. J. Johnston, letter to T. L. McKenney, 24 May 1825, Letters Sent and Letters Received, Michigan Superintendency, Microform 1, Roll 669, Frame 303; W. Clark, letter to J. C. Calhoun, 5 September 1823, Ohio Valley-Great Lakes Ethnohistory Archive.

30. J. Johnston, letter to T. L. McKenney, 11 April 1825, LSLRMS, Microform 234, Roll 669, Frame 428.

31. Ibid.

32. Seneca Chiefs in Ohio, letter to the President of the United States, 15 October 1829, USCSS, Set ID 195, Doc. 47; John Johnston, letter to the President of the United States on behalf of the Seneca Chiefs, 13 December 1828, USCSS, Set ID 195, Doc. 57.

33. Horace S. Knapp, *History of the Maumee Valley: Commencing with Its Occupation by the French in 1680* (Toledo, OH: Mammoth Printing, 1872), 282–3.

34. Henry Howe, *Historical Collections of Ohio* (Norwalk, OH: Laning Printing Co., 1896), 574–5.

35. Lang, *History of Seneca*, 119; Fenton, *Great Law*, 75.

36. Matthew Dennis, *Seneca Possessed: Indians, Witchcraft, and Power in the Early American Republic* (Philadelphia, PA: University of Pennsylvania Press, 2009), 3.

NOTES TO CHAPTER FOUR

1. Seneca Chiefs, letter to President of the United States, In *Council Seneca Village*, 22 September 1830, Correspondence of the Subject of the Emigration of Indians, 170.

2. Annual Report of the Secretary of War (1832), 25–26.

3. C. Vanmeter, letter to Cass, 6 July 1819, Records of the Bureau of Indian Affairs, Microform 1, Roll 7; J. C. Calhoun, letter to John Johnston, 28 April 1820, Records of the Bureau of Indian Affairs, Microform 1, R7; J. Johnston, letter to Cass, 18 September 1827, Ohio Valley-Great Lakes Ethnohistory Archive.

4. Duncan Ivison, *Postcolonial Liberalism* (Cambridge, UK: Cambridge University Press, 2002), 72–73.

5. Donna Haraway, "Situated Knowledges: The Science Question in Feminism and the Privilege of Partial Perspective," *Feminist Studies* 14, no. 3 (Fall 1988): 586.

6. Stuart Hall, "Who needs Identity?" in *Questions of Cultural Identity*, ed. Stuart Hall and Paul de Gay (London, UK: Sage Publications, 1996), 5–6.

7. Stephen Heath, *Questions of Cinema* (Bloomington, IN: Indiana University Press, 1981), 6–7.

8. J. McElvain, letter to T. L. McKenney, 6 November 1829, USCSS, Set ID 195, Doc. 47.

9. Ibid.

10. Seneca Chiefs in Ohio, letter to the President of the United States, 15 October 1829, USCSS, Set ID 195, Doc. 47.

11. Seneca Chiefs, letter to President of the United States, In Council Seneca Village 22 September 1830, Correspondence of the Subject of the Emigration of Indians, Vol. 2, 170.

12. McKenney, letter to P.B. Porter, 2 January 1829, USCSS, Set ID 195, Doc. 57; J. McElvain, letter to S. S. Hamilton, 30 September 1830, Correspondence of the Subject of the Emigration of Indians, Vol. 2, 122.

13. S. S. Hamilton, letter to J. McElvain, 8 October 1830, Correspondence of the Subject of the Emigration of Indians, Vol. 2, 39.

14. To the honorable the Senate and House of Representatives of the United States Congress assembled, 31 January 1831, Correspondence of the Subject of the Emigration of Indians, Vol. 2, 404.

15. J. McElvain, letter to S. S. Hamilton, 10 February 1831, Correspondence of the Subject of the Emigration of Indians, Vol. 2, 409.

16. H. Brish, letter to J. Eaton, 4 May 1831, Correspondence of the Subject of the Emigration of Indians, Vol. 2, 443–5; Niles Weekly Register, 4 February 1826, 369–70.

17. "List of Editors, Proprietors, and persons otherwise connected with the Press, who have been 'Rewarded' by General Jackson," *Daily National Intelligencer*, 27 Sept. 1832.

18. J. Eaton, letter to J. Gardiner, 29 March 1831, USCSS, Set ID 245, Doc. 512, 272–3.

19. United States Department of the Interior, "Treaty with the Seneca," in *Indian Affairs: Laws and Treaties*, ed. Charles J. Kappler (Washington, D.C.: Government Printing Office, 1904).

20. H. Brish, letter to J. Eaton, 14 April 1831, Correspondence of the Subject of the Emigration of Indians, Vol. 2, 425–6.

21. Abstract G, USCSS, Set ID 248, Doc. 512, 122; J. McElvain, letter to L. Cass, 8 December 1831, Correspondence of the Subject of the Emigration of Indians, Vol. 2, 653.

22. Expenditures made by James B. Gardiner, USCSS, Set ID 248, Doc. 512, 121.

23. Seneca Chiefs, letter to J. Eaton, 7 June 1831; J. McElvain, letter to S. S. Hamilton, 12 June 1831, Correspondence of the Subject of the Emigration of Indians, Vol. 2, 471–3.

24. J. McElvain, letter to S. S. Hamilton, 13 January 1831, Correspondence of the Subject of the Emigration of Indians, Vol. 2, 390–1.

25. J. B. Gardiner, letter to L. Cass, 1 December 1831, Correspondence of the Subject of the Emigration of Indians, Vol. 2, 694–7.

26. J. McElvain, letter to L. Cass, 8 December 1831, Correspondence of the Subject of the Emigration of Indians, Vol. 2, 651–4.

27. J. McElvain, letter to S. S. Hamilton, 14 January, 1831, Correspondence of the Subject of the Emigration of Indians, Vol. 2, 390–1.

28. J. McElvain, letter to S. S. Hamilton, 20 September 1830, Correspondence of the Subject of the Emigration of Indians, Vol. 2, 120–1.

29. J. McElvain, letter to S. S. Hamilton, 12 June 1831, Correspondence of the Subject of the Emigration of Indians, Vol. 2, 471–2.

30. S. S. Hamilton, letter to H. Brish, 4 October 1831, Correspondence of the Subject of the Emigration of Indians, Vol. 2, 353–4.

31. J. McElvain, letter to S. S. Hamilton, 17 July 1831, 512.

32. J. McElvain, letter to L. Cass, 15 November 1831, Correspondence of the Subject of the Emigration of Indians, Vol. 2, 684–5.

33. S. S. Hamilton, letter to H. Brish, 4 October 1831, Correspondence of the Subject of the Emigration of Indians, Vol. 2, 353–4. McElvain to S. S. Hamilton, August 1, 1831, CSEI, Vol. 2, 353–4.

34. John McElvain, letter to L. Cass, 7 September 1831, Microform 234, Roll 601; John McElvain, letter to Secretary of War, 15 November 1831, Microform 234, Roll 601; John McElvain, letter to Secretary of War, 1 August 1831, Microform 234, Roll 601; William Clark, letter to Elbert Carring, 20 December 1831, Microform 234, Roll 77; Henry Brish, letter to William Clark, 16 November 1831, Microform 234, Roll 77; William Clark, letter to Elbert Carring, 20 December 1831, Microform 234, Roll 77; Chiefs of the Emigrating Seneca, letter to United States Government, 10 December 1831, Microform 234, Roll 78.

35. W. Clark, letter to E. Herring, 20 September 1831, Correspondence of the Subject of the Emigration of Indians, Vol. 2, 722–3; J. Gardiner, letter to L. Cass, 4 January 1832, Indian Removal Records, L. S. Watson, ed., (Oklahoma City, OK: Histree Publishing, 1985), 15–16.

36. E. Herring, letters to J. McElvain, 6 February 1832, Correspondence of the Subject of the Emigration of Indians, Vol. 2, 757.

37. Seneca of Sandusky Chief, letter to W. Clark, 10 December 1831; Indian Removal Records, 15–19.

38. W. B. Lewis, letter to Henry C. Brish, 22 August 1833; W. B. Lewis, letter to W. Clark, 22 August 1833, USCSS, Set ID 248, Doc. 512, 111.

39. W. Clark, letter to W. B. Lewis, 18 November 1833, USCSS, Set ID 248, Doc. 512, 112–114; Abstract F, USCSS, Set ID 248, Doc. 512, 100.

40. H. Brish, letter to W. Clark, 14 December 1831, USCSS, Set ID 248, Doc. 512, 115.

41. H. Brish, letter to W. Clark, 14 December 1831, Correspondence of the Subject of the Emigration of Indians, Vol. 2, 724–5.

42. Abstract F, USCSS, Set ID 248, Doc. 512, 101, 103–4; J. Gardiner, letter to L. Cass, 4 January 1832; W. Clark, letter to E. Herring, 5 January

1832; Seneca of Sandusky Chiefs, letter to W. Clark, 10 December 1831; Indian Removal Records, 15–9.

43. E. Herring, letter to H. Brish, 22 March 1832, CSEI, Vol. 2, 801.

44. Abstract F, USCSS, Set ID 248, Doc. 512, 101, 103–104.

45. H. Brish, letter to W. Clark, 8 May 1832, USCSS, Set ID 248, Doc. 512, 116.

46. H. Brish, letter to W. Clark, 8 May 1832, Correspondence of the Subject of the Emigration of Indians, Vol. 5, 116; H. Brish, letter to W. Clark, 12 June 1832, USCSS, Set ID 248, Doc. 512, 117, 118.

47. H. Brish, letter to W. Clark, 16 July 1832, USCSS, Set ID 248, Doc. 512, 118.

48. Ibid.; H. Brish, letter to W. Clark, 31 August 1833, USCSS, Set ID 248, Doc 512, 120.

Notes to Chapter Five

1. The situation in Indian Territory is detailed in David La Vere, *Contrary Neighbors: Southern Plains and Removed Indians in Indian Territory* (Norman, OK: University of Oklahoma Press, 2001).

2. L. Cass, letter to W. Clark, 14 July 1832, Correspondence of the Subject of the Emigration of Indians, Vol. 2, 876.

3. Ronald N. Satz, *American Indian Policy in the Jacksonian Era* (Lincoln, NE: University of Nebraska Press, 1974), 137–8.

4. L. Cass, letter to Commissioners, 14 July 1832, Annual Report of the Secretary of War (1832), 32–33.

5. Annual Report of the Secretary of War (1832), 28–30.

6. Ibid, 25–6.

7. Partha Chatterjee, *The Nation and its Fragments* (Princeton, NJ: Princeton University Press, 1993), 6.

8. Annual Report of the Secretary of War (1832), 23.

9. R. Cummins, letter to L. Cass, 22 December 1832, Correspondence of the Subject of the Emigration of Indians, Vol. 2, 576.

10. Charles J. Kappler, "Treaty with the Seneca and Shawnee, 1832," in *Indian Affairs Laws and Treaties, Vol. II*, (Washington, D.C.: Government Printing Office, 1904), 83–385.

11. G. C. Snow, RCIAUS, War Dept. Office of Indian Affairs, Washington, D.C.: [s.n.] (1867), 733–4.

12. Report of William Armstrong, RCAIUS, 1839.

13. C. A. Harris to B. F. Butler, December 1, 1836, annual report 1836, p. 378; Report of W. Armstrong, annual report 1837, p. 583; Report of W. Armstrong, annual report 1838, p. 486; T. Hartley Crawford to W. Armstrong, July 11, 1840, annual report 1840, p. 330.

14. John B. Luce to W. Armstrong, August 1, 1841, Annual Report to commission Indian affairs, 1841, p. 344.

15. Nearly every letter of the Commissioner of Indian Affairs in the nineteenth century remarks on Sandusky Senecas' continued use and development of agriculture and their continued "industry."

16. A resistance to allowing schools and missionaries is noted throughout the 1840s, particularly by Neosho subagent J. Luce, RCIAUS, War Dept. Office of Indian Affairs, Washington, D.C. (1841), 307; Ibid, (1842), 457.

17. B. B. R. Barker RCIAUS War Dept. Office of Indian Affairs. Washington, D.C. (1844), 376.

18. B. B. R. Barker RCIAUS War Dept. Office of Indian Affairs. Washington, D.C. (1845), 527.

19. Andrew Dorn, RCIAUS War Dept. Office of Indian Affairs. Washington, D.C. (1849), 1117; George Mitchell, RCIAUS. War Dept. Office of Indian Affairs. Washington, D.C. (1871) 916–7; Hiram Jones, RCIAUS. War Dept. Office of Indian Affairs. Washington, D.C. (1872), 425, 628.

20. William Armstrong, RCIAUS War Dept. Office of Indian Affairs. Washington, D.C. (1839), 473.

21. William Armstrong, RCIAUS War Dept. Office of Indian Affairs. Washington, D.C. (1841), 317.

22. R.A. Calloway, RCIAUS War Dept. Office of Indian Affairs. Washington, D.C. (1843), 396.

23. B. B. R. Barker, RCIAUS War Dept. Office of Indian Affairs. Washington, D.C. (1843), 428.

24. Ibid.

25. William Armstrong, RCIAUS War Dept. Office of Indian Affairs. Washington, D.C. (1844), 454.

26. Ibid, 469–70

27. Andrew Dorn, RCIAUS War Dept. Office of Indian Affairs. Washington, D.C. (1849), 1116.

28. W. J. J. Morrow, RCIAUS War Dept. Office of Indian Affairs. Washington, D.C. (1851), 401–3.

29. W. J. J. Morrow, RCIAUS War Dept. Office of Indian Affairs. Washington, D.C. (1852), 395.

30. B. A. James, RCIAUS War Dept. Office of Indian Affairs. Washington, D.C. (1849), 152.

31. W. J. J. Morrow, RCIAUS War Dept. Office of Indian Affairs. Washington, D.C. (1852), 394–5.

32. Peter Wilson to William Bouck, August 4, 1843, William Bouck Papers, 2206, New York State Archive.

33. Treaty with the New York Indians. Jan. 15, 1838, 7 Stat. 550; Erminie Wheeler-Voegelin, "The 19th and 20th Century Ethnohistory of Various Groups of Cayuga Indians" (1959), Great Lakes Ohio Valley Ethnohistoric Project Archives, Indiana University Bloomington, 59–66; 72; Andrew Dorn to Unknown, January 2, 1849, RSSIA, M640, R16.

34. Peter Wilson to William Bouck, August 4, 1843, William Bouck Papers, 2206, New York State Archive.

35. H. W. Jones to the Comptroller of the State of New York, December 30, 1857, Quapaw Agency Records, Microfilm Reel 11, Indian Agency Documents, Oklahoma Historical Society.

36. Ibid.

37. Erminie Wheeler-Voegelin, "The 19th and 20th Century Ethnohistory of Various Groups of Cayuga Indians" (1959), Great Lakes Ohio Valley Ethnohistoric Project Archives, Indiana University Bloomington, 63.

38. H. W. Jones to P. Smith, November 11, 1875; Gallien to H. W. Jones, June 15, 1876; W. W. Hawkins to Lucius Robinson, June 13, 1876, Quapaw Agency Records, Microfilm Reel 11, Indian Agency Documents, Oklahoma Historical Society. Carl Albert to Chester Armstrong, March 24, 1956, Carl Albert Collection, Box 24, Folder 66, Carl Albert Congressional Archive, University of Oklahoma.

39. Baptiste to G. A. Colton Esq., May 1, 1862, RCIAUS War Dept. Office of Indian Affairs. Washington, D.C. (1862), 317; Hauptman, *The Iroquois and the Civil War* (Syracuse, NY: Syracuse University Press, 1999), 90.

40. Charles D. Bernholz et al. *"So long as grass shall grow and water run: the treaties formed by the Confederate States of America and the tribes in Indian territory* (Lincoln, NE: University of Nebraska-Lincoln, Center for Digital Research in the Humanities, 2010), 374–85; Laurence Hauptman, *The Iroquois in the Civil War*, 94–95.

41. David C. Hinze and Karen Farnham, *The Battle of Carthage: Border War in Southwest Missouri, July 5, 1861* (New York: Pelican Publishing, 2004), 262; Laurence M. Hauptman, *Between Two Fires: American Indians in the Civil War* (New York: Free Press, 2012), 42; Hauptman, *Iroquois and Civil War*, 94–95.

42. Report of Peter Elder, September 12, 1862, RCIAUS War Dept. Office of Indian Affairs. Washington, D.C. (1862), 287–9.

43. A. V. Coffin to W. G. Coffin, September 25, 1863, RCIAUS War Dept. Office of Indian Affairs. Washington, D.C. (1863), 307–9.

44. W. G. Coffin to W. Dole, September 24, 1864, RCIAUS War Dept. Office of Indian Affairs. Washington, D.C. (1864), 448.

45. P. Elder to W. G. Coffin, September 15, 1864, RCIAUS War Dept. Office of Indian Affairs. Washington, D.C. (1864), 459–60; P. Elder to W. G. Coffin, n.d., RCIAUS War Dept. Office of Indian Affairs. Washington, D.C. (1864), 474–5.

46. D. N. Cooley to J. Harlan, October 31, 1865, RCIAUS War Dept. Office of Indian Affairs. Washington, D.C. (1865), 202.

47. Speech of Isaac Warrior, September 11, 1865, RCIAUS War Dept. Office of Indian Affairs. Washington, D.C. (1865), 505–6.

48. Report of D. N. Cooley, October 30, 1865, RCIAUS War Dept. Office of Indian Affairs. Washington, D.C. (1865), 480–4.

49. William C. Sturtevant, "Oklahoma Seneca-Cayuga," in *Handbook of North American Indians*, Vol. 15, ed. Bruce G. Trigger (Washington, D.C.: Smithsonian Institution, 1978), 541; Velma Nieberding, "Seneca-Cayuga Green Corn Ceremonial Feast," *The Chronicles of Oklahoma* 34, no. 2, (1956) 232–3.

50. James H. Howard, "Cultural Persistence and Cultural Change as Reflected in Oklahoma Seneca-Cayuga Ceremonialism," *The Plains Anthropologist* 6, no. 11, (1961) 23–7; James H. Howard, "Environment and Culture: The Case of the Oklahoma Seneca-Cayuga," *Oklahoma Anthropological Society Newsletter* 18, no. 6, (1970): 5–13; A. C. Parker, "Iroquois Sun Myths," *The Journal of American Folklore*, 23:473–8. October–December, 1910.

51. Howard, "Cultural Persistence," 26.

52. Daniel Heath Justice, "Go Away Water!" Kinship Criticism and the Decolonization Imperative" in *Reasoning Together: The Native Critics Collective*, ed. Craig S. Womack, Daniel H. Justice and Christopher B. Teuton (Norman, OK: University of Oklahoma Press, 2008), 267.

53. Parmenter, *Edge of Woods*, xlv.

54. Timothy J. Shannon, *Iroquois Diplomacy on the Early Frontier* (New York, NY: Viking-Penguin, 2008), 26–7.

55. Parmenter, *Edge of Woods*, xlvi.

WORKS CITED

Abel, Timothy J., and David M. Stothers. "Vanished beneath the Waves: The Lost History and Prehistory of Southwestern Lake Erie Coastal Marshes." *Archaeology of Eastern North America* 29 (2001): 19–46.

Abler, Thomas S. *Chainbreaker: The Revolutionary War Memoirs of Governor Blacksnake*. Lincoln, NE: University of Nebraska Press, 1989.

Abler, Thomas S., and Elisabeth Tooker. "Seneca." In *Handbook of North American Indians*, edited by Bruce G. Trigger. Washington, D.C.: Smithsonian Institution, 1978.

"Annual Report of the Bureau of American Ethnology to the Secretary of the Smithsonian Institution." Washington, D.C.

Aquila, Richard. *The Iroquois Restoration: Iroquois Diplomacy on the Colonial Frontier, 1701–1754*. Lincoln, NE: University of Nebraska Press, 1997.

Axtell, James. "Ethnohistory: An Historian's Viewpoint." *Ethnohistory* 26, no. 1 (1979): 5.

Bangs, Nathan. *A History of the Methodist Episcopal Church, Volume III*. New York, NY: Phillips Lincoln, 1837.

Baughman, Abraham. *History of Seneca County, Ohio: A Narrative of Its Historical Progress, Its People, and Its Principal Interests, Vol. 1*. New York, NY: Lewis Publishing Company, 1911.

Ben-zvi, Yael. "National Appropriations and Cultural Evolution: The Spatial and Temporal Use of Lewis Henry Morgan's Native America." *Canadian Review of American Studies* 33, no. 3 (2003): 211–13.

Blau, Harold. "Dream Guessing: A Comparative Analyis." *Ethnohistory* 10, no. 3 (1963).

Brooks, Lisa. *The Common Pot: The Recovery of Native Space in the Northeast*. Minneapolis, MN: University of Minnesota Press, 2008.

Burton, Clarence Monroe. "Ephraim Douglas and His Times." *The Magazine of History*, 1910, 41.

Butler, General R. "Letter to Maj. Gen. Knox." Records of the Continental and Confederation Congresses and the Constitutional Convention, 11 October 1787.

Butler, General R. "Letter to Major General Henry Knox." Washington D.C.: Continental and Confederation Congresses and Constitutional Convention, 1787.

Butterfield, Consul W. *History of Seneca County: Containing a Detailed Narrative of the Principal Events That Have Occurred since Its First Settlement Down to the Present Time; a History of the Indians That Formerly Resided within Its Limits; Geographical Descriptions, Early Customs, Biographical Sketches, &C., &C., with an Introd., Containing a Brief History of the State, from the Discovery of the Mississippi River Down to the Year 1817, to the Whole of Which Is Added an Appendix, Containing Tabular Views, &C.* Sandusky, OH: D. Campbell & Sons, 1848.

Chakrabarty, Dipesh. "Postcoloniality and the Artifice of History: Who Speaks for 'Indian' Pasts?" *Representations* 37 (Winter 1992): 1–26.

Champagne, Duane. *Social Change and Cultural Continuity among Native Nations.* Lanham, MD: Altamira Press, 2006.

Chatterjee, Partha. *The Nation and Its Fragments: Colonial and Postcolonial Histories.* Princeton, NJ: Princeton University Press, 1993.

Clifton, James. *Being and Becoming Indian: Biographical Studies of North American Frontiers.* New York, NY: Dorsey Press, 1989.

Cole, Charles Chester. *Lion of the Forest: James B. Finley, Frontier Reformer.* Lexington, KY: University Press of Kentucky, 1994.

de le Armand, Richardie "Letter to P. Pierre Potier." In *Les Escrits De Pierre Potier*, edited by Robert Toupin. Ottawa, Canada: Le Presses de l'Université d'Ottawa, 1750.

Deloria, Philip. *Playing Indian.* Yale Historical Publications Series. New Haven, CT: Yale University Press, 1998.

Dennis, Matthew. *Seneca Possessed: Indians, Witchcraft, and Power in the Early American Republic.* Philidelphia, PA: University of Pennsylvania Press, 2009.

Downes, Randolf. *Council Fires on the Upper Ohio: A Narrative of Indian Affairs in the Upper Ohio Valley until 1795.* Pittsburgh, PA: University of Pittsburgh Press, 1940.

Dumond, Isaac. "Speech of Isaac Dumond before the Seneca Pioneer Association." In *History of Seneca County, from the Close of the Revolutionary War to July, 1880: Embracing Many Personal Sketches of Pioneers, Anecdotes, and Faithful Descriptions of Events Pertaining to the Organization of the County and Its Progress*, edited by William Lang. Springfield, OH: Transcript Printig Company, 1880.

Favor, Lesli J. *The Iroquois Constitution: A Primary Source Investigation of the Law of the Iroquois.* Great American Political Documents. New York, NY: Rosen Publishing Group, 2003.

Fenton, William N. *American Indian and White Relations to 1830: Needs and Opportunities for Study.* Williamsburg, VA: Institute of Early American History and Culture, 1957.

———. *The Great Law and the Longhouse: A Political History of the Iroquois Confederacy*. Lincoln, NE: University of Oklahoma Press, 1998.

———. "Northern Iroquoian Culture Patterns." In *Handbook of North American Indians, the Northeast*, edited by Bruce G. Trigger. Washington, D.C.: Smithsonian Institiution 1978.

———. "Problems Arising from the Historic Northeastern Position of the Iroquois, Smithsonian Miscellaneous Collections 100." In *Essays in Historical Anthropology of North America*, edited by Julian H. Steward. 159–252. Washington, D.C.: Smithsonian Institution, 1940.

Finley, James Bradley. *History of the Wyandot Mission*. Cincinnati, OH: The Methodist Book Concern, 1840.

———. *Life among the Indians: Or, Personal Reminiscences and Historical Incidents Illustrative of Indian Life and Character*. Cincinnati, OH: Hitchcock and Walden, 1859.

Foley, Denis. "Iroquois Mourning and Condolence Installation Rituals: A Pattern of Social Integration and Continuity." In *Preserving Tradition and Understanding the Past: Papers from the Conference on Iroquois Research, 2001–2005*, edited by Christine Sternberg Patrick. Albany, NY: The University of the State of New York; The State Education Department, 2010.

Foster, Morris. *Being Comanche: The Social History of an American Indian Community*. Tucson, AZ: University of Arizona Press, 1991.

Foster, Tol. "Of One Blood: An Argument for Relations and Regionality in Native American Literary Studies." In *Reasoning Together: The Native Critics Collective*, edited by Janice Acoose, Craig S. Womack, Daniel Heath Justice, and Christopher Teuton. Norman, OK: University of Oklahoma Press, 2008.

Garraghan, Gilbert J. "St. Regis Seminary—First Catholic Indian School." *The Catholic Historical Review* 4 (April 1918).

Grinde, Donald. "Iroquoian Political Concept and the Genesis of American Government: Further Research and Contentions." *Northeast Indian Quarterly* 6, no. 4 (Winter 1989): 10–21.

———. *The Iroquois and the Founding of the American Nation*. San Francisco, CA: Indian Historian Press, 1977.

Gupta, Akhil, and James Ferguson. "Culture, Power, Place: Ethnography at the End of an Era." In *Culture, Power, Place*, edited by Akhil Gupta and James Ferguson. 9. Durham, NC: Duke University Press, 1997.

Hall, Stuart. "Who Needs Identity?" Chap. Introduction In *Questions of Cultural Identity*, edited by Stuart Hall and Paul de Gay. London, UK: Sage Publications, 1996.

Haraway, Donna. "Situated Knowledges: The Science Question in Feminism and the Privilege of Partial Perspective." *Feminist Studies* 14, no. 3 (Fall 1988).

Hauptman, Laurence. *Iroquois Struggle for Survival: World War II to Red Power*. Syracuse, NY: Syracuse University Press, 1986.

Heath, Stephen. *Questions of Cinema.* Bloomington, IN: Indiana University Press, 1981.

Heckewelder, John. "Letter to Peter S. Du Ponceau, Bethlehem, Pa, 12 August 1818." *Ethnohistory* 6, no. 1 (1959).

Hill, Norman Newell. *History of Knox County, Ohio, Its Past and Present.* Mt. Vernon, OH: A. A. Graham and Company Publishers, 1881.

Hover, John C., Willard K. Wright, Joseph D. Barnes, Clayton Leiter, Walter D. Johns, John E. Bradford, Charlotte R. Conover, and W. C. Culkins, eds. *Memoirs of the Miami Valley.* Chicago, IL: Robert O. Law Company, 1919.

Howard, James H. "Environment and Culture: The Case of the Oklahoma Seneca-Cayuga." *Oklahoma Anthropological Society Newsletter* 18, no. 4 (1970): 5–13.

Howe, Henry. *Historical Collections of Ohio.* Norwalk, OH: Laning Printing Co., 1896.

Huddleston, Duane, Sammie Cantrell Rose, and Pat Taylor Wood. *Steamboats and Ferries on the White River: A Heritage Revisited.* Conway, AR: University of Central Arkansas Press, 1998.

Hunt, George. *The Wilderness Trail.* AuthorHouse, 2004.

Hurt, R. Douglas. *The Ohio Frontier: Crucible of the Old Northwest, 1720–1830.* Bloomington, IN: Indiana University Press, 1998.

Ingham, Sally. "Sketch of Sally Ingham." In *History of Seneca County, from the Close of the Revolutionary War to July, 1880: Embracing Many Personal Sketches of Pioneers, Anecdotes, and Faithful Descriptions of Events Pertaining to the Organization of the County and Its Progress,* edited by William Lang. Springfield, OH: Transcript Printing Company, 1880.

Interior, United States Department of the. "Treaty with the Seneca." In *Indian Affairs: Laws and Treaties,* edited by Charles J. Kappler. Washington, D.C.: Government Printing Office, 1904.

Ivison, Duncan. *Postcolonial Liberalism.* Cambridge, UK: Cambridge University Press, 2002.

Jennings, Francis. *The Ambiguous Iroquois Empire: The Covenant Chain Confederation of Indian Tribes with English Colonies from Its Beginnings to the Lancaster Treaty of 1744.* New York, NY: Norton, 1984.

Johnston, J. "Letter to W.H. Crawford, Secretary of War." Edited by Office of Indian Affairs. Letters Sent and Received D, 6 June 1815.

Jordan, Kurt A. *The Seneca Restoration 1715–1754: An Iroquois Local Political Economy.* Gainesville, FL: University Press of Florida, 2008.

Kaiser, Siegrun. "Munsee Social Networking and Political Encounters with the Moravian Church." In *Ethnographies and Exchanges: Native Americans, Moravians, and Catholics in Early North America,* edited by A. G. Roeber. University Park, PA: Pennsylvania State University Press, 2008.

Kappler, Charles J., ed. *Indian Affairs: Laws and Treaties,* Vol. II, Treaties. Washington, D.C.: Government Printing Office, 1904.

———. "Treaty with the Seneca and Shawnee, 1832." In *Indian Affairs Laws and Treaties, Vol. II*, edited by Charles J. Kappler. Washington, D.C.: Government Printing Office, 1904.

Kelly, John, and Martha Kaplan. *Represented Communities*. Chicago, IL: University of Chicago Press, 2001.

Knapp, Horace S. *History of the Maumee Valley: Commencing with Its Occupation by the French in 1680*. Toledo, OH: Mammoth Printing, 1872.

Lang, William. *History of Seneca County, from the Close of the Revolutionary War to July, 1880: Embracing Many Personal Sketches of Pioneers, Anecdotes, and Faithful Descriptions of Events Pertaining to the Organization of the County and Its Progress*. Springfield, OH: Transcript Printing Company, 1880.

Lévi-Strauss, Levi. *Totemism*. Translated by Rodney Needham. Boston, MA: Beacon Press, 1963.

"List of Editors, Proprietors, and Persons Otherwise Connected with the Press, Who Have Been 'Rewarded' by General Jackson." *Daily National Intelligencer*, 27 Sept. 1832.

MacNeish, Richard S. "Iroquois Pottery Types: A Technique for the Study of Iroquois Prehistory." *Anthropological Series 31* (1952).

McConnell, Michael N. *A Country Between: The Upper Ohio Valley and Its Peoples, 1724–1774*. Lincoln, NE: University of Nebraska Press, 1992.

———. "Peoples In Between: The Iroquois and the Ohio Indians, 1720–1768." In *Beyond the Covenant Chain*. Syracuse, NY: Syracuse University Press, 1987.

McKenney, Thomas, and James Hall. *History of the Indian Tribes of North America*. Philadelphia, PA: Rice and Company, 1872.

Meek, Basil. "Tarhe-the Crane." In *Ohio Archaeological and Historical Collections*, edited by Henry Howe. Columbus, OH: Fred Heer, 1911.

Miller, Susan. "Licensed Trafficking and Ethnogenetic Engineering." In *Natives and Academics: Researching and Writing About American Indians*, edited by Devon A. Mihesuah. Lincoln, NE: University of Nebraska Press, 1998.

Moses, Daniel. *The Promise of Progress: The Life and Work of Lewis Henry Morgan*. Columbia, MO: University of Missouri Press, 2009.

Mulkearn, Louis *George Mercer Papers*. Pittsburgh, PA: University of Pittsburgh Press, 1954.

Nieberding, Velma. "Seneca-Cayuga Green Corn Ceremonial Feast." *The Chronicles of Oklahoma* 34, no. 3 (1956).

Nolan, Emer. "State of the Art: Joyce and Postcolonialism." In *Semicolonial Joyce*, edited by Derek Attridge and Marjorie Howes. 78. Cambridge, UK: Cambridge University Press, 2000.

O'Brien, Greg. "The Conqueror Meets the Unconquered: Negotiating Cultural Boundaries on the Post-Revolutionary Southern Frontier." *The Journal of Southern History* 67, no. 1 (2001).

Ortner, Sherry B. *High Religion: A Cultural and Political History of Sherpa Buddhism*. Princeton, NJ: Princeton University Press, 1989.

Parmenter, Jon. *The Edge of the Woods: Iroquoia, 1534–1701*. East Lansing, MI: Michigan State University Press, 2010.

Peters, John Durham. "Seeing Bifocally: Media, Place, and Culture." In *Culture, Power, Place*, edited by A. Gupta and J. Ferguson. 81–2. Durham, NC: Duke University Press, 1997.

Peters, Richard, ed. *Treaties between the United States of America and the Indian Tribes*. Boston, MA: Charles Little and James Brown Publishing, 1846.

Preston, David L. *The Texture of Contact: European and Indian Settler Communities on the Frontiers of Iroquoia, 1667–1783*. Lincoln, NE: University of Nebraska Press, 2009.

Prucha, Francis Paul. *The Great Father: The United States Government and the American Indians*. Lincoln, NE: University of Nebraska Press, 1986.

Randall, Emilius O. *The History of Ohio, Volume 2*. New York, NY: Century History Company, 1912.

Richard, Peters. *Treaties between the United States and the Indian Tribes*. Boston, MA: Charles Little and James Brown Publishers, 1848.

Richter, Daniel. *The Ordeal of the Longhouse: The Peoples of the Iroquois League in the Era of European Colonization*. Chapel Hill, NC: The University of North Carolina Press, 1992.

Rifkin, Mark. *Manifesting America: The Imperial Construction of U.S. National Space*. London, UK: Oxford University Press, 2009.

Satz, Ronald N. *American Indian Policy in the Jacksonian Era*. Lincoln, NE: University of Nebraska Press, 1974.

Shannon, Timothy J. *Iroquois Diplomacy on the Early Frontier*. New York, NY: Viking-Penguin, 2008.

Shimony, Annemarie A. *Conservatism among the Iroquois at the Six Nations Reserve*. Syracuse, NY: Syracuse University Press, 1994.

Simpson, Audra. "On Ethnographic Refusal: Indigeneity, 'Voice' and Colonial Citizenship." *Junctures: The Journal for Thematic Dialogue* 9 (2007): 67–80.

Snow, Dean. *The Iroquois*. New York, NY: Blackwell, 1994.

Starna, William A., and Robert E. Funk. "The Place of the in Situ Hypothesis in Iroquoian Archaeology." *Northeast Anthropology* 47 (1994): 45–7.

Stocker, Harry E. *History of the Moravian Mission among the Indians on the White River in Indiana*. Bethlehem, PA: Times Publishing Co. Printers, 1917.

Sturtevant, William C. "Oklahoma Seneca-Cayuga." In *Handbook of North American Indians*, edited by Bruce G. Trigger. Washington, D.C.: Smithsonian Institution, 1978.

Thwaites, Reuben Gold, ed. *The Jesuit Relations and Allied Documents*. Vol. 15. Cleveland, OH: The Burrows Brothers Company, 1898.

Thwaites, Reuben Gold, and Louis Phelps Kellogg. *Documentary History of Dunmore's War, 1774*. Madison, WI: Wisconsin Historical Society, 1905.

Tooker, Elisabeth. *The Iroquois Ceremonial of Midwinter*. Syracuse, NY: Syracuse University Press, 1970.

Toupin, Robert, ed. *Les Escrits De Pierre Potier*. Ottawa, Canada: Les Presses de l'Université d'Ottawa, 1996.

Voget, Fred. "Anthropological Theory and Iroquois Ethnography." In *Extending the Rafters: Interdisciplinary Approaches to Iroquoian Studies*, edited by Jack Campisi, Michael Foster, and Marianne Mithun. 347–8. Albany, NY: State University of New York Press, 1984.

———. "Extending the Rafters." (1985).

Vonswearingen, Mr. "Letter to Col. W. Butler." Records of the Continental and Confederation Congresses and the Constitutional Convention, 29 September 1787.

Wallace, Anthony F. C. *The Death and Rebirth of the Seneca*. New York, NY: Vintage, 1972.

Walsh, Martin W. "The 'Heathen Party': Methodist Observation of the Ohio Wyandot." *American Indian Quarterly* 16, no. 2 (Spring 1992): 189–211.

Weibe, Robert. *The Search for Order: 1877–1920*. New York, NY: Hill and Wang, 1966.

Wheeler-Voegelin, Erminie. "The 19th and 20th Century Ethnohistory of Various Groups of Cayuga Indians." Bloomington, IN: Indiana University, 1959.

———. "John Heckewelder to Peter S. Du Ponceau, Bethlehem 12th Aug 1818." *Ethnohistory* 6, no. 1 (1959): 72.

White, Marian et al. "Cayuga." In *Handbook of North American Indians*, edited by William Sturtevant. 500-4. Washington, D.C.: Smithsonian Institution, 1978.

White, Richard. *The Middle Ground: Indians, Empires, and Republics in the Great Lakes Region, 1650–1815*. Cambridge, UK: Cambridge University Press, 2010.

Whittlesey, Charles. *Early history of Cleveland, Ohio, including original papers and other matter relating to the adjacent country*. Cleveland: Fairbanks, Benedict, 1867.

Winter, Nevin Otto. *A History of Northwest Ohio: A Narrative Account of Its Historical Progress and Development from the First European Exploration of the Maumee and Sandusky Valleys and the Adjacent Shores of Lake Erie, Down to the Present Time*. New York, NY: The Lewis Publishing Company, 1917.

Womack, Craig S. "A Single Decade: Book-Length Native Literary Criticism between 1986–1997." In *Reasoning Together: The Native Critics Collective*, edited by C. S. Womack, D. H. Justice and C. B. Teuton. Norman, OK: University of Oklahoma Press, 2008.

Wyllys, Major "Letter to Colonel Harmare." Washington, D.C.: Records of the Continental and Confederation Congresses and the Constitutional Convention, 1787.

Xianqing, Zhang. "The Discourse of 'Tartar': The Proto-Ethnographic Descriptions of Manchu by European Missionaries in the 17th Century." *Academic Monthly (China)* 2 (2009): 1.

INDEX